AF413834

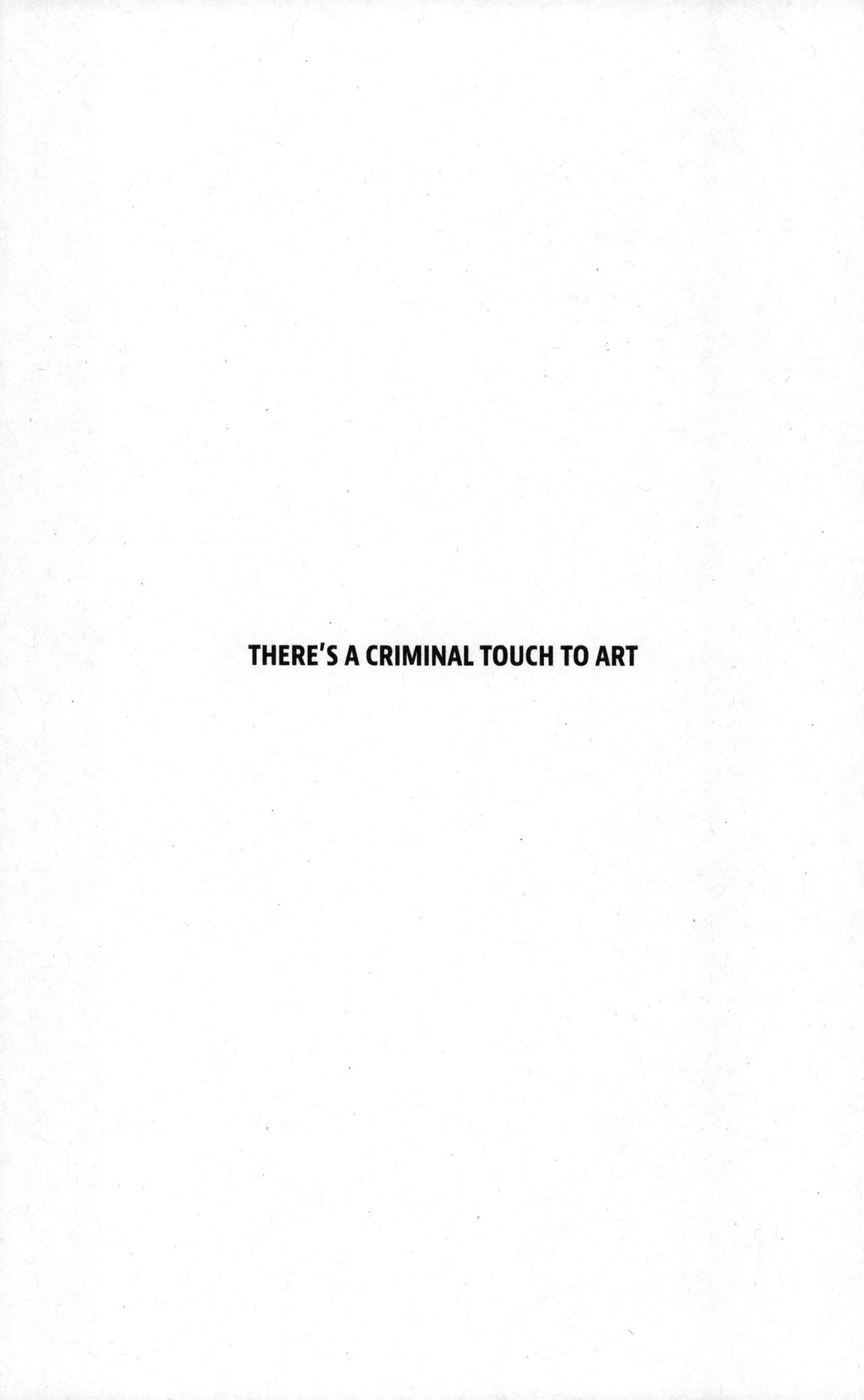

THERE'S A CRIMINAL TOUCH TO ART

THERE'S A CRIMINAL TOUCH TO ART

How **Ulay** Stole Hitler's Favorite Painting
and Redefined Performance Art

–

By **Noah Charney** with
the Ulay Foundation and the Abramović Institute

BLOOMSBURY ACADEMIC

NEW YORK · LONDON · OXFORD · NEW DELHI · SYDNEY

BLOOMSBURY ACADEMIC
Bloomsbury Publishing Inc, 1359 Broadway, 12th Floor, New York, NY 10018, USA
Bloomsbury Publishing Plc, 50 Bedford Square, London, WC1B 3DP, UK
Bloomsbury Publishing Ireland, 29 Earlsfort Terrace, Dublin 2, D02 AY28, Ireland

BLOOMSBURY, BLOOMSBURY ACADEMIC and the Diana logo are trademarks of
Bloomsbury Publishing Plc

First published in the United States of America 2026

A catalog record for this book is available from the Library of Congress.

ISBN: HB: 979-8-7651-6304-7
ePDF: 979-8-7651-6306-1
eBook: 979-8-7651-6305-4

Typeset by Urška Charney
Printed and bound in the United States of America

For product safety related questions contact productsafety@bloomsbury.com.

To find out more about our authors and books visit www.bloomsbury.com and sign up for
our newsletters.

Contents

On the morning of December 12, 1976, Berlin's Neue Nationalgalerie was stunned by an audacious art heist. A painting was stolen during opening hours on that steel-skied, snowy Sunday. Not just any painting—*The Poor Poet* by Carl Spitzweg, reputedly Adolf Hitler's favorite. Within minutes, a call came in. The painting had not been lost, destroyed, or even hidden.

Introduction

It had been rehung, carefully, respectfully, in the modest apartment of a Turkish immigrant family living in Kreuzberg, a working-class district of West Berlin. The caller gave the address and invited the museum to come retrieve it. He was Ulay, a young German conceptual artist with a flair for provocation, performance, and political commentary. The theft was not for profit. It was not even, in the traditional sense, a crime. It was an artwork.

Art theft as art.

This act—at once a theft, a performance, a protest, and a conceptual gesture—would become one of the most famous performance artworks in the history of contemporary art. Titled *Irritation: There's a Criminal Touch to Art*, it was conceived of and executed by Ulay and executed in collaboration with Marina Abramović, his partner in art and life at the time, while being filmed by several others. It was a tightly choreographed disruption of museum culture, a critique of the Nazi residue in the German cultural canon, and a meditation on who has access to art and why. In placing *The Poor Poet* in the home of an immigrant family, Ulay symbolically reclaimed the artwork from a legacy of exclusion and elite ownership, momentarily redirecting it to a more inclusive and deeply human context.

This book is the first monograph devoted to that single, extraordinary action. It tells the full story from three perspectives, each offering a different lens on what took place that day and why it still matters. The first is Ulay's own, drawn from extensive interviews with art historian Noah Charney, conducted before Ulay's death in 2020—most of these recordings were made in December 2015 in Ljubljana, Slovenia. These candid conversations—never before published—offer the artist's direct recollections, motivations, and philosophy behind the act. It is the closest we can come to being inside Ulay's mind on that December morning.

The second perspective is that of Marina Abramović, whose global fame as the high priestess of performance art has only grown in the decades since. As Ulay's partner and collaborator, she brings her own memories and interpretation of the event. Her voice captures not only the planning and execution of the action but also the conceptual underpinnings of it, as well as the emotional and personal stakes of such a high-wire act of public provocation. But as she herself describes it, recollections even of eyewitness events can differ. She refers to the Kurosawa film *Rashomon*, which shows conflicting, very different eyewitness accounts of the same crime.

The third strand is that of Charney himself, who contextualizes the action both as an artistic milestone and as a deeply subversive engagement with the idea of possession, legality, and the institutional frame through which we view art. Charney, who has written extensively on art crime and art history, guides readers through the symbolic terrain that Ulay and Abramović traversed, from the cultural memory of Hitler's aesthetics to the marginalization of immigrants in postwar Europe and from the sanctity of museum walls to the radical proposition that theft, too, can be art.

This approach means that this book brings together three perspectives: Ulay (posthumously), Abramović, and Charney. In practice, Ulay and Abramović each told their stories to Charney, who wrote them up, before adding his own chapters to the story. Chapter 4 is Ulay's direct account. Chapter 5 is Abramović's. The other chapters were written by Charney.

Though Ulay and Abramović created dozens of influential works together and apart, *Irritation* remains Ulay's most iconic solo work, and it was one in which Abramović had both a key role and a front-row seat. Its power lies not only in its brazenness but also in its layered intentionality. It was neither a stunt nor a prank. It was a carefully orchestrated act with complex symbolic payloads and engaging themes of ownership, nationalism, memory, and justice.

In the decades since, the artwork has acquired a near-mythic status in performance art circles, frequently cited but never deeply examined—until now. This book is, in a sense, a corrective to that neglect. It is also a precious first-person account from two titans of contemporary art, a must-have for any archive or library that covers the subject. It invites readers not only to relive the events of that day but also to think critically about what art can be and where its limits lie. Can a theft be art if it leaves no material trace, only a conceptual residue? Can the museum—a bastion of elite culture—be productively challenged, even momentarily upended, by a single symbolic gesture? And what does it mean to take art out of a gallery and place it in a family's home, however briefly?

By weaving together the first-person voices of the artists with historical and critical analysis, this book provides a multifaceted portrait of a single, unforgettable act. It explores the collaborative dynamic between two of the twentieth century's most influential artists (one of whom continues to work at the highest level) at a time when they were just beginning to shape the boundaries of performance art. It offers fresh insights into the intersection of aesthetics and activism, of politics and poetics, of crime and creativity.

This is the definitive account of *Irritation: There's a Criminal Touch to Art*, a moment when art left the museum, crossed a legal line, and found new meaning on the other side—entering as a key chapter in the story of art.

THE BERLIN LIFTING

A very ugly, highly suspicious matte black van idles across from the Neue Nationalgalerie in Berlin. The engine stays on. Out steps a tall, slender man in a graphite-colored *Kleppermantel*—a raincoat that blends into the winter light like a shadow. He strides into the museum.

At the coat check, he sheds the raincoat. In his pocket are a pair of wire-cutter pliers. He descends to the basement.

Beyond a glass climate-control barrier, he stops. In front of him hang three modestly sized Romantic-era paintings by Carl Spitzweg. One of them, *The Poor Poet*, is an icon—instantly recognizable to any German who came of age in the mid-twentieth century. But there's a guard. Too close. Too alert. He'll need to go.

On the opposite wall is a painting of chess players. The slender man shifts in front of it. Then, without warning, he begins to laugh—loudly, maniacally, unhinged.

The guard approaches. He glances at the chess painting. "What's so funny?"

The man doesn't answer. His heart is pounding. In a flash, he pivots, bolts to *The Poor Poet*, clips the wire with his pliers, rips the painting from the wall, and runs.

The alarm screams to life.

He blasts through the climate barrier, races up the stairs, and dashes through the foyer. The entrance is choked with people waiting to get in. He weaves through them and crashes through the emergency exit, the stolen painting clutched tight under his arm.

Snow slaps his face as he sprints toward the black van. He slips—hard—on the ice. A guard yells, "Now we get him!"

But he's up. Running again.

The van is locked tight—except the driver's side, held ajar by a wad of chewing gum. He yanks it open, throws himself in, slams the door, and locks it. A guard grabs the handle—too late.

The van lurches forward.

He's gone. Free and clear, one assumes.

If it sounds like the opening of a thriller, maybe it should be. But it's not fiction. This is a firsthand account from the performance artist Ulay, describing what he called "the Berlin lifting"—formally titled *There's a Criminal Touch to Art*, a 1976 theft-as-performance.

Ulay is in Berlin because Marina Abramović, his partner in life and art, is performing a solo piece there. While waiting for her show, he visits the Neue Nationalgalerie, expecting modern art. Instead, in the basement, he finds a quiet shrine to nineteenth-century German Romanticism. And there, on the wall, is *The Poor Poet*—a painting that resonates with him instantly.

It's not something most non-Germans would recognize. Its fame owes more to its dubious distinction as one of Hitler's favorites. Painted in 1839, it shows an old poet in tattered clothes, lying under a shredded blanket, composing verse in a freezing garret. An umbrella plugs a hole in the ceiling. His quill is clenched between his teeth. To stay warm, he feeds scraps of paper—including his own writings—into a small tiled stove. It's charming, ironic, quietly tragic. Like O. Henry's "Gift of the Magi," the poet must destroy what gives his life meaning in order to go on living.

Ulay remembers this image vividly—it was the only color reproduction in a book he was given as a child. That personal memory, combined with the painting's place in postwar German cultural memory, makes it a symbol of deep contradiction. Small enough to tuck under an arm, heavy with historical baggage. It becomes his "trigger."

He begins planning.

The idea was to stage a performance that ties together four incongruous elements: Berlin's elite institutions (the Neue Nationalgalerie and the Akademie der Künste [or Academy of Arts]); the DAAD artist residency at the Künstlerhaus Bethanien; and the marginalized, heavily Turkish neighborhood of Kreuzberg. Ulay calls Kreuzberg "shabby, ugly, ghetto-like"—home to immigrants treated as disposable labor by the postwar German economy.

He spends a week casing the museum—what criminologists call "hostile surveillance." He doesn't want to rely on high-tech gear. "I wanted to do everything with my hands and feet," he says.

The gallery's security is tight. The painting is wired; removing it triggers an alarm. The revolving doors at the entrance lock automatically if the alarm goes off. But fire regulations offer a loophole: The emergency exits flanking the entrance can't be locked—they're only sealed.

"So I thought," Ulay recalls, "to break the seal off the emergency exit and push that door open—that would be my escape."

And it was.

—

Ulay wants the performance documented. Abramović is already inside the Neue Nationalgalerie before he enters, stationed with a Super 8 camera—one roll of film loaded, another in her pocket—ready to capture the moment from within. Ulay has plotted every detail with his gallerist, Mike Steiner, who promises to cover any legal fallout. Arrested mid-action or after, it doesn't matter—Steiner says he'll handle it.

Finding someone to film an actual crime, though, proves nearly impossible. Eventually, Ulay persuades Jörg Schmidt-Reitwein, a gifted cinematographer who's worked with Werner Herzog. But even he keeps his distance—he agrees to follow the action in a separate car, never stepping out, maintaining a thin wall of automotive metal between himself and the felony unfolding.

—

Saturday, December 11, 1976. Ulay drafts a document he calls "the action"—a fourteen-step recipe, a conceptual blueprint for what's about to happen. Alongside it is a sketch of a triangular diagram linking three cultural institutions—the Neue Nationalgalerie, the Akademie der Künste, and the Künstlerhaus Bethanien. From the last point, an escape arrow juts outward—into secular society.

He mails the plan to the media. It won't arrive until Monday—after the fact.

To complete the theater, he photographs *The Poor Poet*, blows it up to poster size—5 x 7 feet—and prints it on linen. On Sunday morning, the day of the heist, he drives to the Akademie der Künste and mounts the reproduction over its entrance, blocking it entirely.

The escape vehicle? A hideous matte black van, formerly used by French police, straight out of the 1968 Paris uprisings, that has been his and Marina's home for weeks—they have no fixed abode and were sleeping either in the van or in an artists' hotel run by Ulay's Berlin gallerist, Mike Steiner.

The look is deliberate. At the time, Germany is gripped by fear of domestic terrorism, and Ulay wants something as conspicuously shady as possible. The van looks like trouble. Unfortunately, it acts like trouble too. That morning, it refuses to start. He has to push it in second gear to get it going.

Not exactly the ideal getaway ride.

—

Now, sweating, breathless, with the stolen Spitzweg riding shotgun, Ulay barrels through Berlin toward Kreuzberg. Police? Not his biggest worry. It's the cabdrivers. "I knew they listened to the police radio for fun," he says. "And they liked to help. They'd block the roads themselves."

The van is too distinctive to hide. That's the point—but it also makes Ulay an easy mark.

He makes it to Kreuzberg. Parks. Grabs the painting. He's brought a nylon bag to conceal it—but the painting doesn't fit. "It was bigger than I thought. Not big, but with this baroque frame, it was very heavy."

So he tucks it under his arm and runs.

Passing a Neue Nationalgalerie exhibition poster, he stops just long enough to pull out a smaller reproduction of the Spitzweg, which he pins over the existing image—another layer of visual mischief—then bolts down the street.

He's already been scouting potential collaborators in Kreuzberg. One Turkish family agrees to help. He hasn't told them about the theft. "I said we were shooting a documentary, and could we borrow their ambiance, just to hang a painting while we film."

Schmidt-Reitwein, energized by the moment, abandons his car and follows, camera bouncing against his shoulder.

Before Ulay enters the apartment, he ducks into a phone booth and makes a call—a move few criminals would consider. He calls the museum. He asks to speak with Professor Dieter Honisch, the director. "I wanted to say: Listen, I've stolen the painting. I want you to come and verify it's unharmed. That's all. I'll accept the consequences."

But the police have already taken over the lines.

So he tells them instead. Gives them the address. Invites them to come retrieve the painting.

Then he heads upstairs.

Second floor. He rings the bell. A woman opens the door, children at her side. He steps inside. No hammer. No nails. So he takes one of their paintings off the wall and hangs *The Poor Poet* in its place.

And then, the wait.

"I was completely freaked out," Ulay recalls. "Cold, chain-smoking, snow falling. I was waiting for the consequences."

He doesn't know what will happen. He hopes the act is seen for what it is—a protest, not a threat—but German law may not be in a playful mood.

About twenty minutes later, the street is sealed off. The police arrive. They don't know what they're walking into. A prank? A trap? Or something even stranger: an artist turning himself in?

Two men approach. One wears civilian clothes. The other is Professor Honisch. "This is my assistant," Honisch says, then leans in and whispers, "He's actually a police officer."

Honisch seems sympathetic.

He examines the painting. It's unharmed. Ulay states he's willing to take full responsibility. He's escorted back to the Neue Nationalgalerie and seated in Honisch's office.

"I made a statement," Ulay says. "This was a demonstrative action, not a theft in the traditional sense." Not a performance, exactly, either—but a political protest. Against the institutionalization of art. Against the marginalization of immigrants. Against a system that polishes cultural trophies while ignoring social decay.

He's still jailed for the night.

One phone call. He calls Mike Steiner.

Steiner, elated, is already celebrating. Champagne flows. Meanwhile, Ulay lies in a cold cell.

—

The next morning, he's hauled into court. The prosecutor reads out a list of charges. Ulay's stomach drops. "I saw myself in prison for a really long time."

But the judge seems calm. Young. Quiet. Sympathetic.

When the prosecutor finishes, the judge asks Ulay to explain the event in his own words. Ulay begins, "This was a demonstrative action . . ."

But before he can finish, the courtroom door bursts open. A man storms in, shouting a name. The judge responds instantly: "Karl!" They're old friends. This is Ulay's lawyer, sent by Steiner.

Whether it's the personal connection or the weight of Ulay's story, the judge sides with him. The prosecutor wants a full trial. Ulay's foreign citizenship complicates things—he was born in Germany but is living in Amsterdam as a Dutch citizen.

A formal trial is scheduled for three months later.

Ulay never returns.

"No one did," he says.

The trial proceeds without him. The court hands down a sentence: thirty-six days in jail or a fine of 3,600 Deutschmarks.

"I never had that kind of money," Ulay says. But it hardly matters.

He's long gone.

The Spitzweg returns to its rightful wall. The museum moves on.

And Ulay?

He walks away.

Well, almost.

—

And what about the fallout?

The headlines waste no time. One paper declares, "A Fool Steals a Painting." Another frames it as the act of a "leftist radical" desecrating "our most beautiful painting." The story floods the press. Tabloids and right-wing outlets brand Ulay a criminal, a threat. The left-leaning and more serious publications, though, recognize it for what it is: a bold, unsettling commentary on art, power, and exclusion.

Meanwhile, the footage survives.

Schmidt-Reitwein's 16mm film captures the action from his trailing car—a documentary-style fragment of the theft as it unfolds in real time. And Abramović? She pulls off a quiet coup of her own. Despite having never shot film before, she manages to capture a few precious seconds from inside the gallery, hidden in plain sight, under the nose of security.

"I'd positioned her in the basement," Ulay later explains. "Showed her how the camera worked. She couldn't see very well, had no experience. But the roll lasts three minutes and shoots eighteen frames per second. She ran it to the end, took the film out, swapped in the second roll, and stashed the used one—in her boots or her bra, I don't know. We'd rehearsed it. Because I knew: If the police showed up and saw someone with a camera, they'd seize it."

They do.

The police confiscate the camera and, with it, the fresh, unexposed film—thinking they've secured the only record.

But Abramović's smuggled reel makes it out. It only holds three seconds of usable footage, but it's gold. When edited together with Schmidt-Reitwein's external shots, those few seconds become something more: not just a record of a crime but a lasting artifact of a performance that's part protest, part heist, part myth.

A fool steals a painting?

No. A radical reclaims a symbol.

And leaves just enough behind to make sure no one forgets it.

But that's only part of the story. And one side of it. For more, we'll turn to Ulay's own word-for-word account, followed by Abramović's. Then we'll pick up the endgame of the story and look at it in the context of the story of art/theft.

chapter 2

HITLER'S FAVORITE PAINTING

It's not Spitzweg's fault that he made Hitler's favorite painting. It's a cheesy, Romantic, saccharine one, but it does what it set out to do well. It might not be a masterpiece, but it's interesting and well executed and it has been effective for millions of people. It also happens to be infamous.

—

There is a certain delight in art that plays its wit subtly. It doesn't shout, doesn't scandalize, doesn't require a PhD in semiotics to interpret. It smiles to itself, quietly, like a man reading poetry under a blanket in an unheated attic. If that image feels specific, it's because it is: *The Poor Poet*, Carl Spitzweg's most iconic work and arguably the most beloved painting in German history. It is also the visual embodiment of the Biedermeier aesthetic—at once modest, humorous, and deeply human.

Carl Spitzweg was not meant to be an artist.[1] Born in 1808 in Unterpfaffenhofen, near Munich, he studied pharmacy, trained in chemistry, and worked as a pharmacist before taking up painting in his late twenties. A self-taught artist, he began sketching during his convalescence from illness, and this private hobby would eventually morph into a professional identity. Spitzweg never aligned himself with the grand schools or radical manifestos of the nineteenth century. Instead he trained his attention on the small, the quiet, the overlooked—subjects that made him the unlikely poster child of the Biedermeier style.[2]

Biedermeier is less a movement than a mood. It emerged in the years following the Napoleonic Wars, roughly from 1815 to 1848, during a time of political repression and domestic retreat in the German-speaking lands. The Congress of Vienna restored monarchies and imposed reactionary governance.[3] Artists and intellectuals responded not with revolution but with a turn inward—to the household, the local, the humble. It was a culture of private life: of piano recitals in parlor rooms, porcelain figurines, and watercolor still lifes.[4]

Biedermeier art is often accused of being sentimental or even escapist. It is, but that judgment misses its quiet radicalism. In a time when public expression was constrained by censorship, Biedermeier art explored inner freedom. It celebrated the quiet dignity of the domestic sphere, the poetry of small pleasures, the absurdities of everyday life. Spitzweg was its visual bard.

His paintings are intimate, jewel-toned vignettes of bourgeois and petit-bourgeois life: the absent-minded botanist tumbling into a stream, the nervous suitor climbing a balcony, or the Sunday painter perched on a hilltop. They are funny without being cruel, sympathetic without being saccharine. They remind us that there is narrative value—and artistic merit—in the ordinary.

Nowhere is this more evident than in *The Poor Poet* (*Der arme Poet*), painted in 1839. The work measures a modest 14 by 18 inches—roughly the size of a laptop screen—and yet it contains an entire universe.[5] We see a man, presumably a poet, lying on a thin mattress in a frigid attic. The ceiling slopes, the wallpaper peels, and a single stove struggles to warm the space. The poet appears unconcerned. Clad in a red cap and reading a manuscript, he counts meter with one hand and clutches his papers with the other. Above him hangs an umbrella to catch drips from the leaking roof. Sheets of rejected poetry smolder as kindling near the stove.

The humor is gentle but unmistakable: The poet is so poor he burns his own verse for warmth but so committed to his art that he continues writing amid absurd conditions. There's an almost monastic quality to his devotion—he is the secular saint of art for art's sake.

Spitzweg's genius lies in how much he communicates through domestic detail. The absurd umbrella, the dog-eared papers, the nearly empty cupboard: Each object builds the character's world without the need for narrative explanation. It is a portrait not of a particular man, but of an archetype—the starving artist, noble in his suffering, laughable in his obstinacy, beloved in his earnestness.

The painting was immediately popular. It spoke to a middle-class public that both romanticized and pitied the artistic life. It has been reproduced on postcards, calendars, postage stamps, and even cigarette cards. During the Third Reich, *The Poor Poet* became so entrenched in the cultural psyche that Adolf Hitler reportedly declared it his favorite painting.[6] That it was admired by both performance artists and fascist dictators might suggest the image's deep ambivalence. Like all great icons, it is open to projection.

—

Adolf Hitler's taste in art has long fascinated and disturbed historians, collectors, and cultural critics. It offers a window into the mind of a man who aspired to remake European culture according to a personal aesthetic that was, paradoxically, both romantic and regressive. Among the artworks Hitler most admired was *The Poor Poet* which perfectly embodied the kind of sentimental, nationalist, and antimodernist values Hitler cherished. But his interest in art went far beyond private admiration. As a failed artist himself, Hitler harbored a complex relationship with the art world: one of resentment, longing, and, ultimately, ruthless control.

The Poor Poet was a favorite of Hitler's not simply because of its technical skill or domestic charm. Though humorous and melancholic, the image struck a deep chord with Hitler. It portrayed the archetype of the misunderstood genius, unrecognized by a decadent society—a narrative Hitler believed mirrored his own failed attempt to gain admission to the Akademie der bildenden Künste Wien (Academy of Fine Arts in Vienna). The painting also celebrated humble, distinctly German values: frugality, intellectual seriousness, and the noble suffering of the solitary creator. Hitler reportedly kept a reproduction of *The Poor Poet* with him during his military service in World War I and spoke of it with admiration throughout his life.[7]

As a young man, Hitler aspired to become an artist. He applied twice to the Vienna Academy and was rejected both times, largely due to his poor figure drawing skills.[8] Ironically, his watercolor landscapes, many of which survive today, were not technically incompetent. They were tidy, if uninspired—charming cityscapes, Alpine vistas, and architectural studies that reflect a decent command of perspective and a love for classical symmetry. What they lacked in originality, they made up for in technical correctness. This was the standard by which Hitler would later judge the entire canon of art: not by innovation or intellectual daring but by skill, order, and conformity to a romantic ideal.

When Hitler rose to power, he turned his long-simmering resentments into policy. As part of the Nazi cultural machine, he sought to purge Germany of what he called "degenerate art"—essentially all modernist movements from Expressionism to Dadaism, which he viewed as Jewish, Bolshevist, and corrupt. In 1937, the Nazis mounted the infamous "Entartete Kunst" (Degenerate Art) exhibition in Munich, showcasing works by artists such as Kandinsky, Klee, and Kirchner in chaotic arrangements with mocking labels.[9] Meanwhile, just down the road, Hitler's approved art was on display in the Great German Art Exhibition. This juxtaposition was no accident: It was a manifesto of aesthetic and ideological war.[10]

Hitler's ultimate vision for German art culminated in the plans for the "Fühermuseum" in Linz, Austria.[11] Intended as the greatest museum in the world, this enormous neoclassical complex was to house the finest examples of European painting from antiquity through the nineteenth century. It would enshrine the cultural superiority of the German people and serve as a personal monument to Hitler's tastes. Linz, his boyhood hometown, was to be transformed into a cultural capital to rival Paris and Rome.

To fill the museum, Hitler employed art historians, curators, and SS officers to acquire—or, more often, seize—artworks from across Europe. Jewish collections were targeted first: The Rothschilds in France and Austria, the Schloss family, and countless others lost masterpieces to Nazi plunder. Works by Rembrandt, Vermeer, Titian, and Rubens were prioritized, as were German and Austrian painters such as Altdorfer, Friedrich, and Spitzweg. The Einsatzstab Reichsleiter Rosenberg (ERR), a special Nazi task force, coordinated massive art seizures in occupied territories, often using forged documentation or forced sales under duress.[12]

In total, Hitler's agents amassed thousands of paintings, many of which were never returned to their rightful owners. The so-called Nazi gold train and hidden salt mine caches like those in Altaussee, Austria, became infamous for the treasures they concealed.[13] Some of these works were destined for Linz; others were earmarked for top Nazi officials or sold to fund the war. The Linz museum itself was never built, but Hitler reviewed architectural models and floor plans obsessively, often placing paintings on imaginary walls.

What is striking about the art Hitler favored is not just its traditionalism but its ideological function. His selections exalted the Volk, glorified rural life, upheld classical beauty, and rejected ambiguity or abstraction. It was art as propaganda—beautiful, yes, but above all obedient. In this sense, *The Poor Poet* stood as more than a nostalgic favorite. It was, to Hitler, a kind of self-portrait: the unappreciated genius who would one day remake the world.

Yet even in this, there is irony. *The Poor Poet* was painted by Spitzweg, an artist who was gently satirical and intellectually playful, and who belonged to the Biedermeier tradition, a style that cherished domestic life and individual contemplation over grand political narratives. Spitzweg never imagined his work would be coopted into the ideological machinery of fascism. But coopted it was, like so much else.

In the end, Hitler's taste in art reflected the same qualities that defined his rule: rigid, exclusionary, sentimental, and ultimately tragic in its consequences. The Linz museum remained a fantasy, an unrealized temple to a distorted aesthetic. But the damage his tastes inflicted—through censorship, theft, and cultural erasure—was devastatingly real. And at the center of this complex and contradictory story sits *The Poor Poet*, quietly counting the meter of a poem, as the world around him burned.

—

It is worth pausing on this point. In a century when German art swung from Romanticism to Expressionism, from Bauhaus clarity to postwar abstraction, *The Poor Poet* remains disarmingly old-fashioned. It is figurative, anecdotal, and small scale. And yet it endures, perhaps because it captures a timeless truth: the artist who endures hardship, who is misunderstood or overlooked, and who creates because he must. This is an archetype that transcends its Biedermeier roots.

Spitzweg never courted the avant-garde. He was more comfortable sketching caricatures than manifestos. But there is a quiet modernity in his insistence on the ordinary. In a way, his paintings foreshadow the work of later artists like Edward Hopper or even the narrative comics of Chris Ware—artists who find the sublime in the mundane.

Carl Spitzweg died in 1885, still beloved but never canonized among the greats. He was too modest, too humorous, and too accessible. And yet his legacy lives on not only in museum collections but also in the visual language of everyday life. Walk through a Berlin flea market and you might see a copy of *The Poor Poet* in a cracked frame or printed on a linen tea towel. It is kitsch, yes—but it is also sincere.

In the end, Spitzweg reminds us that there is no shame in small stories. There is beauty—and irony—in imperfection. Art does not always need to shock or disrupt. Sometimes it only needs to notice.

As the poet in the attic teaches us, even when the roof leaks and the fire burns your best work, you keep writing.

And it was a hit. Spitzweg would paint three versions. One is housed at the Munich Pinakothek. One is in a private collection, its location unknown publicly. The third is the one that Ulay stole.[14] But it is still missing. It was stolen, you see. Just not by Ulay.

chapter 3

ULAY AND ABRAMOVIĆ

I first met Ulay at a dinner party thrown by Slovenia's most famous rock star. The musician's wife prepared salt-baked fish, and as she cracked open the crust, I felt the gush of a groupie as I looked through the steam at Ulay, a man I had studied in art history class, now sitting across the table from me. Ulay had married a beautiful Slovenian woman and settled down on the sunny side of the Alps, in Ljubljana.

Ulay was one of just a handful of living artists who are enshrined in most "Introduction to Art History" textbooks. You can find him in the last chapter, after you've combed over Lysippus and Giotto, Donatello and Michelangelo, Ingres and Picasso. There he is, usually in conjunction with his onetime, long-term romantic and artistic partner Marina Abramović. Their work as a duo was seminal to the course of performance art in the late 1970s and 1980s, but they were also great artists in their separate careers. Ulay began as one of the few official photographers for Polaroid in the 1960s. While we think most often of his performance art (he always preferred the German word *aktion*, or an action rather than a performance), most iconically his 1976 art theft as artwork, the subject of this book, he actually began as a photographer. His independent career also touched upon shifting genders, decades before this was à la mode. He invented a hybrid-gendered alter ego, Renais Sense, for which he made up one hemisphere of his face like a woman and the other like a man. He was a pioneer in body art, considering the body to be the artistic medium par excellence.

Indeed, just last night, when, as it turns out, he was dying, I was writing about him for a forthcoming book, featuring him in a chapter on shock as an artistic tactic. With Abramović, he explored the human body and its functions as artistic acts. In *Imperonderabilia*, one of the most famous performance artworks of all time, he and Abramović stood, naked, in a narrow doorway within a gallery, forcing visitors to shimmy past them, sidling sideways, confronting either his nakedness or hers, in order to access the gallery space. Early works as a duo included a performance in which they took turns slapping each other, interested in the sound this made. In another work, they repeatedly ran, naked, smashing into columns in a parking garage with their shoulders. The columns were unattached and had been rigged on sleds, so they would slide ever so slightly backward with each strike. But they were heavy and caused bruising nonetheless. Later works examined the physical capabilities of the human body other than pain. *Nightsea Crossing* (1981–1987) was a series of twenty-two performances over a total of ninety days in which the two artists would sit opposite each other, completely still, for many hours at a time. Both practiced Ayurvedic meditation and trained extensively for these performances, which required incredible concentration and mental strength. In extensive interviews I undertook with Ulay, he explained how they trained themselves to "scratch itches with our minds." The errant fly, not to mention audience members who made a game of trying to distract them (the way tourists might try to make a Buckingham Palace guard move from their rock-still stance), were among the obstacles.

Ulay and Abramović will always be intertwined, even though they eventually had a falling-out (which I reported in *The Guardian*).[1] After the lawsuit, the two met by chance, or fate, at an Ayurvedic retreat in rural India. Ulay was there with his talented wife, designer Lena Pislak, who was his constant companion, support, and driving force for years. But what could have been very awkward was not. The two artists decided to put the issue aside and became friendly again, against all odds. Years later, they even discussed writing a joint memoir together.

After his split with Abramović, Ulay continued to work and cultivate relationships with a younger generation of artists, curators, gallerists, and people like me, an art historian. Artist JAŠA performed with Ulay in New York in 2016. *Cutting Through the Clouds of Myth* was Ulay's first performance after a hiatus of more than twenty-five years, and it was much anticipated, no more so than by his collaborator, an artist almost half his age. "His focus, his presence was a unique experience."

There was a fatherly guru vibe about him. When he would email or text me, he would call me "Dear." He took up activist causes, calling himself an "artivist" for clean water. He spoke poetically, eloquently, with the sort of phrases that you want to jot down, or carve in stone, falling like water from his lips, even in casual conversation. He once said, "One can learn many things in life, but not art. The madness you need—the must which is shaking you all the time. You are an artist even when you are asleep. Because of the must." He was an artist to the bone.

His legacy will be kept illuminated by the Ulay Foundation, which opened in 2019 in Ljubljana. It includes a gallery space and will host residencies for artist couples.

"My entire artistic practice," Ulay said, "is rooted in the belief that art has the capacity to contribute to life." The goal of his foundation is to continue his legacy and support others who use art to contribute to life.

Ulay was, above all, a man of enormous warmth and kindness. I spent countless hours at his kitchen table in his sunny Ljubljana apartment, sharing his Marlboros and drinking a special healthful brew, which he liked to call his magic potion, that Lena prepared for him. We had planned to write a book together but never found the time to finish it. He had beaten cancer twice already (once documented in the film *Project Cancer*). Each time, he had gone on an Ayurvedic retreat and that, combined with the help of the respected oncology clinic in Ljubljana, had sent his cancer into remission. Against all odds, with the loving support of those closest to him, he remained remarkably active, even in sickness. He said, "Death is the ultimate answer. But life is absolute."

At one time he had considered his illness and the documentation of it as a type of performance.

It would be his ultimate *aktion*.[2]

Before we move on to Ulay and Marina's accounts of the 1976 action, it would be wise to spend some time getting to know them and their oeuvre, both together and individually, beyond the basic introduction you just read.

ULAY: THE BODY AS ART, THE LIFE AS LEGACY

Frank Uwe Laysiepen—better known to the world as Ulay—was a singular presence in the art world, a figure both mythic and real, who helped define the contours of performance art while steadfastly refusing to be defined himself. Born in Germany in 1943, Ulay began his artistic life not with the radical actions that would later define his legacy but behind a camera. A gifted photographer, he was among the first officially sponsored by Polaroid in the 1960s, a period during which he explored the artistic potential of the instant photograph, from handheld devices to studio-size cameras. His photographic practice, though often overshadowed by his later works, remained a cornerstone of his creative identity.

But it was when he left behind a conventional life—including his family and his commercial photography studio—and relocated to Amsterdam that Ulay fully embraced the avant-garde. There he transitioned from image maker to image, becoming both medium and message in a series of radical performance pieces that carved out his place in art history. His early solo work already suggested his fascination with gender, identity, and the body. In the *(S)he* series, he transformed himself into a hybrid-gendered alter ego, Renais Sense, dividing his face vertically—half man, half woman—a meditation on duality that predates contemporary conversations about gender fluidity by decades.

In the world of performance art, the body is not merely a tool, it is the artwork. Ulay believed this deeply. His performances were not rehearsed scripts or easily consumable spectacles—they were physical, emotional, often painful explorations of endurance, presence, and human connection. In the late 1970s, he met Marina Abramović, and for the next twelve years, they would form one of art's most intense and productive duos, inextricably linked both romantically and artistically. Together they redefined the boundaries of what art could be.

Their collaborations were fearless. In *Imponderabilia* (1977), the pair stood naked in a narrow gallery doorway, forcing visitors to squeeze sideways between their bodies. Another piece featured the two repeatedly running into opposite walls, the impact moving the freestanding columns and bruising their bodies in tandem. In *Nightsea Crossing* (1981–1987), a series of twenty-two durational performances across ninety days, Ulay and Abramović sat opposite each other in complete stillness for hours at a time, training themselves to reach extreme levels of mental control—scratching itches with their minds, as Ulay once put it.

Even as their joint fame rose, Ulay maintained a separate, independent voice. One of his most powerful solo actions was *There Is a Criminal Touch to Art* (1976).

Yet while Abramović's star rose higher in the 2000s—boosted by a major MoMA retrospective and the documentary *The Artist Is Present*—Ulay's name remained most revered among those in the know: artists, historians, and curators. His presence in art history textbooks, rare among living artists, was secured not through mainstream fame but by the enduring significance of his work.

Despite—or perhaps because of—his cult status, Ulay largely resisted the traditional gallery system. For decades, he declined representation by major galleries, choosing instead to chart his own course. He did what he wanted, never chasing wealth or notoriety. This independence lent his work a purity, a raw sincerity that endeared him to a new generation of artists and thinkers.

In 2012, Ulay was diagnosed with cancer. True to form, he initially conceived of the illness as a kind of final performance. The resulting documentary, *Project Cancer: Ulay's Journal from November to November* (2014), directed by Damjan Kozole, offers an intimate glimpse into this period. Part film diary, part retrospective, the documentary follows Ulay through chemotherapy, meetings with old friends and collaborators, and a journey through his past works and philosophies. While the temptation to frame cancer as another *aktion* was there, the gravity of the illness grounded the experience in stark reality. As he recovered, he reflected not on death but on life. The film ends with Ulay gazing from the terrace of his home, saying, simply, "This is beautiful." And then, to the camera, "You are beautiful."

Remarkably, he beat the disease. Twice, in fact. Each time, thanks in part to Ayurvedic treatments and the care of doctors in Ljubljana, where he lived with his wife, the designer Lena Pislak, Ulay emerged with renewed vitality. With Lena as his constant companion and creative ally, he embraced what turned out to be a renaissance period. He returned to the stage, to the gallery, to the world. In 2016, he performed *Cutting Through the Clouds of Myth* in New York, his first live action in more than twenty-five years, in collaboration with Slovenian artist JAŠA. A new generation of artists looked to him not only as a legend but as a mentor—a "fatherly guru," as one collaborator put it.

During this final act, Ulay finally accepted gallery representation with MOT International and began receiving the institutional accolades long due. His work was featured at Art Basel, his Polaroids shown in Rotterdam, and a major exhibition was planned at Kunsthalle Frankfurt. A previously unauthorized video of his emotional reunion with Abramović during her MoMA performance went viral, watched by millions. The world was finally paying attention again. And Ulay, now in his eighth decade, was glowing.

Through it all, he remained remarkably humble. To friends, he signed emails affectionately. He believed that art should be in service to life, not ego. He took up activist causes, calling himself an "artivist" and championing access to clean water. His final major endeavor was the founding of the Ulay Foundation in Ljubljana. The foundation preserves his legacy and hosts residencies for artist couples, embodying his belief in the transformational power of creative collaboration.

When Ulay passed away in 2020, the art world mourned not only a titan of performance art but also a gentle, poetic soul whose work continues to pulse with vitality.

He lived his life as he performed: intensely, sincerely, and fearlessly. His work made people uncomfortable, made them laugh, and made them think. It confronted taboos, physical limits, and emotional vulnerabilities. But above all, Ulay's art invited people to *be present*—with him, with themselves, and with each other. That, in the end, may be his greatest gift.

As he once said, "Death is the ultimate answer. But life is absolute."

And Ulay lived absolutely.

MARINA ABRAMOVIĆ: BETWEEN PRESENCE AND PAIN

The first time I met Marina Abramović was in a hotel room in Ljubljana. There was no fanfare, no entourage, no sense that one was in the presence of arguably the most famous living artist in the world. She was down to earth, thoughtful, warm, and deeply unimpressed with herself. She described herself, with a smile, as "just a Balkan grandmother," a phrase delivered with such disarming humility that it immediately dissolved any art world intimidation. What struck me then—and stayed with me—was her profound sense of purpose. She radiated the kind of calm intensity that suggests a person who has lived many lives within a single lifetime and who sees no contradiction between greatness and groundedness.

Marina was born in Belgrade, Yugoslavia, in 1946, into a family of Yugoslav partisans turned Communist Party royalty. Her upbringing was rigid and severe—her mother imposed curfews into her thirties—but the intensity of her early life seeded a kind of creative radicalism. When she began making art in the 1970s, she was already veering toward what would become her signature mode: live performance, centered on her own body, pushing herself to extremes of endurance and vulnerability. She would become known as the "grandmother of performance art," though the epithet fails to capture the searing energy, even danger, in her work.

In the early days of performance art, the medium was fringe, strange, even laughable to many in the art world. But Abramović was never interested in accessibility. She was interested in truth—especially when it was uncomfortable. Her early solo works established her fearlessness: In *Rhythm 10* (1973), she stabbed the spaces between her fingers with a knife as fast as possible, repeating the sequence while playing back a recording of the first attempt. In *Rhythm 0* (1974), she placed seventy-two objects—some benign, others lethal—on a table beside her and invited the audience to use them on her body however they wished. For six hours, she stood still as her clothes were cut off, her skin was cut, and a loaded gun was pointed at her head. She did not move. Her only rule was that she would take full responsibility for everything that happened.

"I am the object," she said.

This willingness to surrender control, to expose herself completely to time, pain, and others, would become the core of her artistic philosophy. But it was when she met Ulay that a new chapter began. Their romantic and artistic partnership, from 1976 to 1988, remains one of the most legendary collaborations in art history. Together they created a body of work that examined love, ego, conflict, physicality, and presence in ways that no one had before or has since.

Their first meeting was electric. As Abramović tells it, she met Ulay in Amsterdam, on the very day of her birthday, and instantly knew their lives would be intertwined. Within weeks, they were living together in a Citroën van, traveling Europe, making work on the road. They were, in every sense, partners—mirroring each other, challenging each other, building a shared identity that blurred the line between life and art. They were so synchronized that they often dressed identically, cropped their hair in matching styles, and referred to themselves as a two-headed body.

Their performances as a duo were often physically demanding, emotionally raw, and meticulously rehearsed through a kind of monastic discipline, with works like the aforementioned *Relation in Time* (1977),

Imponderabilia (also 1977), and *AAA-AAA*, when they screamed into each other's mouths, locked in a crescendo of shared catharsis.

But it wasn't all pain. There was a fierce, strange tenderness in their work—an intimacy so intense it was sometimes hard to watch. In *Breathing In, Breathing Out* (1977), they sealed their mouths together and passed breath back and forth until they nearly asphyxiated. In *Rest Energy* (1980), Abramović held a taut bow while Ulay pointed the arrow directly at her heart. The slightest tremble could have been fatal. Both performances were choreographies of trust, proof that art could be both conceptual and deeply emotional.

Their final work together, *The Lovers: The Great Wall Walk* (1988), was a literal and symbolic goodbye. They each began at opposite ends of the Great Wall of China and walked toward each other, meeting in the middle after ninety days and 2,500 kilometers. There they embraced and parted ways, both personally and professionally. The piece was supposed to culminate in a wedding. Instead it became a poetic breakup, a farewell performed on the scale of myth.

In the years that followed, Abramović emerged as the undisputed face of performance art. Her solo career blossomed. With major exhibitions, retrospectives, and a 2010 MoMA show that drew lines around the block, she transformed her once-marginal medium into a global phenomenon. The documentary *The Artist Is Present*, which chronicled the MoMA performance of the same name—where she sat silently, for 736 hours, inviting museum-goers to sit across from her—catapulted her into a new level of public consciousness. She was no longer a radical Balkan outsider; she was an icon.

Yet even as she reached these heights, the memory of Ulay lingered—for her, and for the public. During *The Artist Is Present*, Ulay appeared without warning, taking the seat opposite her. In a now-famous clip that has gone viral many times over, she opened her eyes and, upon seeing him, instantly teared up. They grasped hands, and nothing else needed to be said. It was the purest kind of performance: unrehearsed, spontaneous, and human. Millions watched it online, many not knowing the backstory. For those who did, it was a moment of sublime resolution.

But their postseparation relationship was not without pain. There was the lawsuit. And yet life surprised them again. The two ran into each other unexpectedly at an Ayurvedic retreat in rural India. What could have been awkward became an opening. They spoke. They forgave. They even discussed the idea of writing a joint memoir. It never materialized, but the gesture alone spoke volumes.

Abramović has often said that pain is transformative, that art must be felt in the body to be real. Her work with Ulay embodied this belief. Their relationship—tumultuous, beautiful, transcendent—was both the source and the subject of some of the most important art of the twentieth century. In many ways, they made each other. Their combined legacy is larger than either could have built alone.

And yet Abramović has always been more than a partner in a famous duo. She is a philosopher of presence, a mystic of the body, and a conjurer of silence. She sees art not as an object to be viewed but as a force to be lived. Her entire practice is an invitation—to slow down, to witness, to sit with discomfort, and to confront mortality and memory. She created the Marina Abramović Institute to continue these ideas, fostering a new generation of performance artists and thinkers. Even as her fame has grown, she has never stopped challenging herself—or us.

When I think back to that first meeting in Ljubljana, to her laugh, her honesty, and her lack of pretension, I'm reminded that greatness need not come adorned. It can come in the form of a Balkan grandmother, sipping tea in a hotel room, telling stories of love and loss, of walls walked and breaths exchanged.

Marina Abramović's art asks us to be present. To sit still. To feel time. And in doing so, she has changed how we understand what art—and life— can be.

WHEN ARTISTS COLLIDE: THE ULAY–ABRAMOVIĆ LAWSUIT AND ITS LEGACY

Few artistic partnerships in history are as iconic—or as emotionally and creatively entwined—as that of Marina Abramović and Ulay. From 1976 to 1988, they were collaborators, lovers, muses, and coconspirators. Their boundary-breaking performances, ranging from physical endurance pieces to acts of trust and intimacy, left a permanent mark on the history of performance art. But when their relationship ended, a new question emerged: How would they navigate their shared legacy?

For years, the answer seemed to be amicably. Though they didn't speak from 1988 until 1999, both artists continued their independent careers and maintained mutual respect for the work they had created together. That changed in the early 2010s, when tensions over credit and compensation escalated into a lawsuit that surprised the art world.

In 1999, encouraged by gallerist Sean Kelly, Ulay and Abramović signed a detailed contract outlining how to manage their coauthored works. Ulay sold Abramović the physical archive of their collaborations, which she could use to create prints and reperformances. In return, she agreed to provide regular sales reports and divide net proceeds from any commercial use: 50 percent to galleries, 30 percent to herself, and 20 percent to Ulay. Their agreement also specified how they would be credited—"Ulay/Abramović" for works made from 1976 to 1980 and "Abramović/Ulay" for works made between 1981 and 1988—reflecting their evolving contributions and artistic profiles over time.

According to Ulay, the contract was not consistently honored. He reported receiving only a few royalty payments over the course of sixteen years and claimed many sales went unreported. Of greater concern to him was the matter of artistic credit. In several reperformances and exhibitions, he alleged that his name was omitted entirely, a painful erasure for someone whose identity was interwoven with the work.

From Abramović's perspective, the situation was more complex. Her fame had grown exponentially after her 2010 MoMA retrospective *The Artist Is Present*, followed by a well-received documentary of the same name. With new commercial ventures, high-profile collaborations, and the founding of the Marina Abramović Institute, she had become the face of performance art to a global audience. The administrative burden of maintaining her archive and keeping track of every contractual obligation was immense. That she failed to provide regular reports to Ulay was not necessarily out of malice but perhaps due to a mix of oversight and the relentless pace of her expanding career.

Importantly, Abramović did not contest the existence or terms of the contract. When Ulay took the matter to court in Amsterdam, she chose not to escalate the dispute with public counterattacks. The legal process unfolded quietly and professionally. In September 2016, the court ruled in Ulay's favor, ordering Abramović to provide accurate accounting, restore proper attribution to coauthored works, and pay a sum related to past royalties. The court found that Ulay's moral and economic rights had been violated but did not suggest that Abramović had acted out of vindictiveness.

To her credit, Marina complied fully with the court's ruling. She acknowledged the outcome and made the necessary adjustments. What could have devolved into a bitter public feud instead became a closed chapter—albeit one with scars on both sides.

It's important to note that the lawsuit was not about money alone. At its heart was something more personal: recognition. For Ulay, the works they made together were the high point of his career and the foundation of his artistic identity. To see those works exhibited without his name or reshaped for commercial purposes without his knowledge was deeply painful. For Marina, who had spent the subsequent decades building a towering solo career, it may have been easy to overlook the nuances of that early partnership in the midst of her global rise.

And yet this story is not one of villains and victims. It is a story of two people who shared something profound, fell apart, and spent decades negotiating what that shared past should mean in the present. In many ways, it was inevitable that tensions would arise. Theirs was no ordinary collaboration; it was a total fusion of life and art. Untangling it was never going to be easy, but there were moments of grace.

In the end, the lawsuit served a useful purpose. It clarified roles, affirmed boundaries, and allowed Ulay to reclaim his rightful place in the story. And it reminded the art world that even those whose lives appear larger than life are human—capable of missteps, miscommunications, and, most of all, reconciliation.

Marina remains a towering figure in contemporary art, and rightfully so. Her vision, discipline, and daring have inspired generations. Ulay, too, has left an indelible legacy—quietly, with humility, and now with the clarity that legal affirmation can bring. Their work together changed the face of performance art. Their story, complex and human, is part of that legacy.

This book is now a continuation of their legacy together. All is healed, only mutual admiration and affection remain. This is a testament to this.

chapter 4

ULAY'S ACCOUNT OF THE ACTION

THE PLAN

Marina was invited to do a performance in Berlin at the Künstlerhaus Bethanien, and after our collaboration I started already with the first joint performance in Venice in June 1976. I drove with her to Berlin and she had an unfinished cycle of works that were called the *Rhythm* series, *Rhythm 0, Rhythm 1, Rhythm 5*, et cetera, and this was one of the last performances that she wanted to execute as a solo work.

There I took photographs of the performance. This is a publication from Bildsand, and Bild is a Boulevard Press, a very well-known, rightist Boulevard Press. That was published in the paper. So I took photographs of her action; that's how I came to Berlin. Then, while in Berlin and preparing her performance, I went to the Neue Nationalgalerie. To my surprise, in the basement of the Neue Nationalgalerie—the Neue Nationalgalerie is actually supposed to show modern art, late modernist art—there was a section of German Romantic Biedermeier painting, mid-nineteenth century.

And to my even bigger surprise, there was a painting by Carl Spitzweg, the German painter, called *The Poor Poet*.

It's a painting that I was educated with because it was the only color reproduction in my reading book in the first grade of school. It's a very Romantic painting. Later on, Tomek Ebeli analyzed the painting; it's very interesting in the book, the first act. But at the same time, I got information from the DAAD. [This is short for Deutscher Akademischer Austauschdienst, or the German Academic Exchange Service, which was a powerful and progressive force in the international art and academic scenes, particularly through its Berliner Künstlerprogramm, Berlin Artists-in-Residence Program, which began in 1963.] And they have ateliers for artisan residents in Berlin, in the Kreuzberg neighborhood, in Künstler Hospital. Künstler Hospital used to be a British hospital, then it was used for artist-in-residence and art programs.

I wrote a pamphlet, an introduction of the DAAD, and made quite a point that the reason why I wanted to invite foreign artists for the artists-in-residence program was to stimulate Berlin's cultural program and arts scene.

And then for some reason I made a relation between DAAD, Künstlerhaus Bethanien [a renowned art center in Berlin known for its international residency program and exhibitions], and the Neue Nationalgalerie. How could I possibly link these cultural institutions without including also the Academy of Arts [established in 1695], where students learned about the history of art and how to make it?

So I came up with this idea overnight. If I do something and connect all these institutions, that would be a statement. But to connect it with what and why? And then I went to Kreuzberg, and I found there quite a large community of Turkish migrant workers.

Kreuzberg was completely run down and was shabby and ugly, a terrible ghetto-like place. The Turks were discriminated against, but the Turks of course were attracted to do the dirty jobs between the 1950s and 1960s. Then I thought, well, you know, to bring the three institutions, the Academy of Arts, the Neue Nationalgalerie, Künstlerhaus Bethanien, to bring those together and then escape into the secularized society part, the part where the Turkish migrant workers lived. But I need a trigger for this, you know, to get something going, something very annoying and irritating that would trigger the whole thing. And therefore I decided to steal a Spitzweg painting, which is really like a German identity icon.

I thought, well, if I bring this image, the painting from the institutions, and bring the Spitzweg painting into the living quarters of a Turkish immigrant family and hang it there, that will do.

And so I had about a good week to study everything because you know I wanted to do everything with my hands and feet, not with high-tech equipment and assistance and stuff like that.

I also got in touch with Mrs. Wilma Kottusch, the filmmaker, engaged a cameraman called Jörg Spitzer-Reitwein. And there was Mike Steiner, my gallerist, who was the producer of the whole action, including legal consequences, providing me with a lawyer and such. This was the team. More about them later.

I started at the Neue Nationalgalerie, studying the possible escape, getting out. I checked and the paintings were all wired; that means if you touch a painting, an alarm goes off inside and outside the museum. The main entrance is two revolving doors. They would block, so you can't get out. But aside from the two revolving doors are emergency exits and they can't be locked. They're sealed only by fire brigade or whoever.

So I thought, well, to break the seal open and push the fire door open, that would be the escape.

THE HEIST

On Sunday, December 12, 1976, I drove with my car to the Academy of Arts. And I had, prior to this, made a photographic reproduction of the Spitzweg painting, about two meters by one meter fifty, on photographic linen. It's a huge blow-up, like a balloon.

So first I went to the Academy of Arts and would block the entrance with this huge reproduction. It was a Sunday, so no one would be there.

On the Saturday before, I had made a concept from the action, a short statement: the action I described in fourteen stages, and I made a drawing, like a little pyramid. One institute, the other institute, the third institute, that was a triangle, and then from there I escaped outside the courtyard section.

I had sent this on Saturday to the media, before I actually did it. So either they were sloppy or didn't notice it or didn't pay attention to it or they did not work on Sundays. I was expecting that to happen, that's why I sent it on Saturday. I expected that there would be no reaction, neither interference holding me up or nor arresting me prior to doing it.

From the Academy of Arts, I drove with my van at the time—that was this incredibly ugly van, typical for the 1968 Paris Revolution, the sort used by the French police. It was painted matte black, it was an incredibly ugly car, corrugated iron, and painted muddy black. A very suspicious kind of a vehicle, especially in this time when, in Germany, there were a lot of terrorist activities, like the Second of June Movement, the Red Army Faction, things like this.

I drove from the Academy of Arts in the direction of the Neue Nationalgalerie. I parked the car behind the Neue Nationalgalerie. I left it with a running engine because when I started on Sunday morning with this action, I had a flat battery. So we were pushing the car and had to put it in second gear to get it running. This meant that I had to park the car close to behind the Neue Nationalgalerie, but leave the running engine—hopefully the engine would keep going on!

I went into the Neue Nationalgalerie with a coat, and I left my coat on in the gallery's coat check hall. I had a plier—only one plier—and the plier was to cut the wire behind where the painting was hung. I walked into the museum with a very typical German raincoat. It's an amazing coat. I never wore it again. I left the coat at coat check. And then I went down to where the painting was.

The Neue Nationalgalerie is a gigantic foyer, it's gigantic, and then you have stairs going down to the basement. And there you have two very big climate-controlled doors, very big, because the paintings, the German Romantic paintings section had to be climatized—temperature, humidity, et cetera, et cetera. And there was the painting. There were three specific paintings. One was the one that was for my plan.

Marina was there, taking pictures for me as I had been taking photographs of her performance. I had given her my Super 8 camera and two rolls of film. One is in the camera and one she had in her pocket. I had her sitting or standing down in the basement in front of the two climate-control doors. They're just to shoot a few seconds of material—if I make it. If I have the painting, run with the painting under my arm, rush through the two climate-control doors and fly up the stairs, that is just three seconds. She did it. I positioned her there, I explained how to use the camera, because she'd never made film or photos.

And then I said, "The film is three minutes. The Super 8 film is eighteen images a second, it's about three minutes." So she wandered through filming until the end of the roll, took it out, put a new roll in, and put the one with the film on it in her boots. And I prepared that, too, because I knew if the police come and see people with cameras, they'll come immediately to confiscate the cameras in case they contain evidence.

Down in the basement by the Spitzweg there was a guard in the back and there was a guard very much in the front, and I had to get rid of the guards. Opposite the Spitzweg painting was another painting in which people were playing chess. So I stood in front of this painting and started laughing very loudly.

Then the guard came and stood beside me and looked at the painting and asked what was so funny. I walked around him, grabbed the Spitzweg opposite, cut the wire, ran out of the two climate-control doors, was flying up the stairs, through the foyer, where there were three hundred people because it was on a Sunday, rushed to the emergency exit, got out with the painting under my arm and ran toward the car.

I had such an adrenaline rush that I fell. It was snowy. I fell and then I heard the guards, there were three guards on my heels outside. Then I heard one of the guards screaming, "Now we get him! Now we get him!" I got an extra booth of adrenaline, got on my feet, kept on running, and got to the car.

I'd locked all the doors to the car but not the door to the driver's side, because I knew that if maybe I was just about to make it, they might tear open the door and they'd grab me. So in I went and locked the driver's side door too. It was close.

So I got in the car, put the painting beside me, closed the door, and yes, there was already one guard holding onto the handle of the door. But it was locked, and the engine was running. Fortunately.

I accelerated and got away.

THE GETAWAY

Then I had to drive about, I think from the Neue Nationalgalerie to Künstlerhaus Bethanien in Kreuzberg, it's maybe a drive of ten minutes. The problem was, I knew that taxi drivers enjoy listening to police radio. That's fun for them. So they'd know that the police were looking for my car. But my car is so easy to recognize. And I knew that the taxi drivers could block the roads to help the police, as they sometimes did, especially in that terrorist time. So I had to, as soon as possible, get rid of the car and continue without it.

Just entering the district of Kreuzberg, I put the car in a parking space, grabbed the painting under my arm, and started running with the painting. I went running to Künstlerhaus Bethanien. In the car, I had a nylon bag in which I wanted to put the painting, but the painting was much bigger than I'd thought. The painting is actually not big, but its Baroque framework was, and it was very heavy. So I couldn't put it in the bag. But the bag had the poster with a color reproduction of the painting in it.

So I was running to Künstlerhaus Bethanien with the painting under my arm. I pinned this color reproduction of the same painting over posters advertising the Neue Nationalgalerie exhibition. Once that was done, then I ran in the direction of the Turkish family. I had been visiting several Turkish families, but one was willing to collaborate.

I didn't say anything about a stolen painting, I'd said that we are making a documentary film and was it possible that we use the ambiance, the environment, your environment, just to hang the painting briefly while we make film shots, and so on. They said, "Yes okay, no problem." So they didn't know.

Before I went up, in the house and up to the apartment, from a public phone, right in front of the house, I called the museum. I wanted to talk to Professor Dieter Honisch, who was the director of the museum at the time.

I wanted to tell him, "Listen, I have stolen the painting. If you come here I want you to come and just testify that I have not damaged or destroyed the painting. That's all. And then I take all consequences."

But because in such a case the police take it all over, I didn't get to him. Instead I got the police on the phone. And so then I went up and hung the painting.

I went in there and rushed up to the second floor, rang the bell. They opened the door, the lady with a couple of children around her. I went in there. I didn't have a hammer and nails, so I took one of their paintings off the wall and I hung this stolen painting on the wall in its place. That was it.

Then I went down waiting for action, for the police to arrive. I was completely freaked out.

I was cold. I smoked one cigarette after the other. It was snowing. It was so miserable. And I was waiting for the consequences. I gave the police the address, where, etc. After maybe twenty or thirty minutes, police trucks sealed off the whole block. They didn't care about me, as I was standing there smoking, they just sealed off the whole block. And then, after some time, a great Mercedes-Benz came with two men in it. The driver and then Professor Dieter Honisch, the director. The driver introduced himself as the assistant of Professor Honisch. But then Honisch turned around to me and said, "Good news."

Then they went inside and looked at the painting and he said what he could see by his eye: that the painting is not damaged, it's not destroyed, there is no damage to it.

And then I said, "I'll take the consequences, take me with you."

I got in the car, and they drove me back to the Neue Nationalgalerie. We were sitting in his office, with two others I think, and I made a statement that this was a demonstrative action, not a theft in the traditional sense that I want in riches.

Then they put me in prison.

In Germany, you have a law where they can put you for twenty-four hours in prison and you have to be brought to a judge or first with a prosecutor.

So I was in prison. I could make one call and I called Mike Steiner from the prison, the gallerist, who had promised me, if you undergo the action and get arrested, I will take care of a lawyer for you. He said it was all ready, and I said, "Okay, I hope so." One phone call, I said, "Mike, you better get a lawyer, I have a hearing tomorrow and you better get a lawyer." He said, "Don't worry, I'll get you a lawyer."

THE CONSEQUENCES

Well, the authorities had a drink of champagne for the success of the day and so did my team, without me. I was in prison. And the next day I was led to a small courtroom with a judge, civilians, and a prosecutor. And the prosecutor started reading a list of crimes, I don't know how you call this in English.

I was not prepared for that at all. I was not prepared that a prosecutor had such a list of crimes that he was putting on me. The judge was rather young and was cool, quiet. And when the prosecutor had finished reading the list of accusations, the judge started talking and wanted me to give my own interpretation of it. Why? He said, "It's a demonstrative action." Then the door opened, somebody came into the courtroom. I didn't know who, but the man who came in shouted a name in happy greeting, I think, "Ernst!"

The judge replied with enthusiasm, "Carl!"

What the fuck was he doing?

They had been student friends. And that was my lawyer, this Carl.

The judge saw the whole action and interpreted the action, due to my explanation, as I would have hoped, and completely differently than what the prosecutor said. It looked like I'd gotten very lucky.

The only problem was that I had Dutch citizenship, and I was living in Amsterdam, and of course there will be a court case and there would be a trial here in Berlin. But because I lived outside Germany, in the Netherlands, they had a little bit of problem of whether I would come to the trial or not, if I would take the consequences. Three months later was a trial date at the court in Berlin, and I was given, I think, thirty-six days imprisonment or a fine of 3,600 Deutschmarks (about $9,000 in today's money) or something like that. I never had so much money at one time back then, so there was never a question of whether I could pay it.

So three months later there was a trial at the court in Berlin. I would face this imprisonment then or have to pay the bail.

I didn't go. Nor did I pay nor did anybody else.

THE MESSAGE

Of course, Mike Steiner's gallery was the producer of this, which we could later call *Irritation—Da ist eine kriminelle Berührung in der Kunst* (*Irritation: There Is a Criminal Touch to Art*). And there was a writer, a leftist intellectual in Germany called Günter Wallraff. [Wallraff was a renowned German investigative journalist known for his undercover reporting techniques. His methods involved assuming false identities to expose social injustices, particularly those affecting marginalized groups. Ulay's action has been described as being executed in a style reminiscent of Günter Wallraff's investigative approach. This comparison highlights the performance's intent to challenge societal norms and bring attention to the experiences of immigrant communities in Germany.]

Now Günter Wallraff approached my gallerist and said, "Can we make a fake press conference and only invite real journalists?" Mike Steiner was contacting the *Bild Zeitung* newspaper, and Günter Wallraff was in the gallery, together with a friend who had tape-recorded everything. In the gallery space there was a gliding door maybe for office space and so he was behind it and peeped a little, so he was there for the press conference.

So it was a fake press conference, including two or three people from *Bild Zeitung*. *Bild Zeitung* had, on the Monday after the action [December 13, 1976], a front page that read: "Leftist Radical robbed our most beautiful painting." Later that day the headline ran.

I do not refer to it as a performance. It was a protest action, *aktion*, first of all, against the institutionalization of art; secondly, about discrimination against foreign workers; and thirdly . . . you know, West Berlin at the time was like a . . . a preemie.

If you were living in East Germany and you were, at the age of eighteen, to be drafted, you could move to West Berlin, and you would be exempt and on top they would pay you to move and I think you have tax advantages to keep that thing [West Germany] artificially alive.

So I mean the whole West German policy, the Cold War, the East German, the Socialist thing, et cetera, et cetera, the Turkish War, the institutionalization of the art—there were so many things that were eventually touched on.

Bild Zeitung had printed the next day, when they got to hear that this was a demonstrative action, that I was not a terrorist, I was not a left-wing radical, and I'd given back the painting. They changed the whole thing to a new narrative: A fool had stolen the painting.

Then it went in the regular daily paper, then it went into better papers, then it went into magazines and art magazines and it was more investigated, with writers asking what was the demonstrative point about this action? And there is a lot written about it, really.

OOPS

One year later, around November or December, we were at a friend's house in Wiesbaden. Michael Berger, he's a collector. And this part of the year was so miserable. The roads were frozen, there was ice, everything was ice and frozen. We were miserable, poor, still living in our van, in the back. And we said, "We need some sun." And that was Marina, me, and Joe Jones, a Fluxeum artist. [Fluxeum was a private museum in a deconsecrated church dedicated to experimental art and the Fluxus movement—Ulay and Marina had an early joint performance there in 1978.]

So he just said, "Okay, I'll get you tickets. You go to where you want to go. I've got an idea: Morocco."

He brought us to Frankfurt and we got on a plane. We had a little pot of pocket money, but he paid for the tickets.

We went on the plane and we had a stopover at Munich airport. We had to get out off the plane and for some reason they caught me! They didn't have computers at the time, they just had the black book with the bad guys' names in it, and they caught me and arrested me there. And then I served those thirty-six days' imprisonment or I had to pay the 3,600 Deutschmarks fine. I thought I'd gotten away with it!

So I called Michael Berger again, from Munich, and I said, "Michael, I have a big problem."

He loved it, actually. He just loved it. But I had a big problem, you know. I'd been arrested again. Either thirty-six days' imprisonment or I must pay the fine, you know.

And he said, "Okay, I have a brother in Munich. He'll come to the airport and he's going to pay the fine." So we had some money with us, we handed it over to the police, but it was not enough. I said, "Okay, we wait for Mr. Berger, the brother, and Michael Berger to pay the rest."

So that was it. About a year exactly to the day after the action.

I think that the German jurisdiction also had approached the German embassy in Holland. I do remember that I got a call, a letter actually, from the consul in Amsterdam that I must appear before the consul and talk about it.

I was divorced in Germany, but I didn't pay child support, because I had no money, I couldn't pay (I was living in the back of an ugly van!). So there was a social debt I owed, not a criminal debt. I had to go to the consulate, talk with the consul, and say, "I'm sorry, I'm a poor artist, I can't pay it."

He said, "That's no good, sooner or later you they'll get you."

And he was right. At one stage I passed a Dutch/German border, they took me off the train, I got arrested, and they put me in a terrorist prison. It was like a Fort Knox. And I was there, convicted for social neglect.

I think I was about ten or fourteen days in prison. The worst part is that I didn't know for how long. So I got really nasty to the world. But yeah, it was a great meditation time. It was maybe the time that I read the most books in my life.

THE FILM

We go back to the planning and filming.

Remember Marina had changed the film in the gallery before the police arrived, as was taught her. She changed the film and put the exposed film in her boot or bra, and there was the unexposed film in the camera. And then she went up to the main ground floor of the gallery. Of course, there was chaos. Because police asked everybody, what did the man look like? Some said one meter sixty and blond, others said he was two meters tall and green! Everybody different.

And she was filming actually through the glass when the police came. They came with several trucks, a lot of police came; from the museum she filmed them arriving. And then of course they took the camera. And then they took out the film. But she had the film of the heist itself. That had been safely hidden. So it could be added to the Wilma Kottusch film to make this short movie, which we would call like the action, *Irritation—Da ist eine kriminelle Berührung in der Kunst*, and show it at the Sixth International Forum of New Cinema during the Berlin Film Festival.

Gallerist Mike Steiner had been working for some time as an artist in New York. He did minimalist paintings, which I liked. Then he decided to open a video gallery, which was very early. There was one person only in Germany, Gerry Schum. He had a truck with video equipment and would drive from artist to artist, artist-made video recordings, very early. [Fernsehgalerie Gerry Schum was founded in Berlin in 1969, but Schum died in 1973.]

And since Mike Steiner was one of the very first video galleries that means he would attract video artists and in particular female performance artists, feminists. That was pretty great, and Mike had a hotel, he owned the Mike Steiner Artist Hotel in Berlin. That's where he made money.

Mike had invited Marina and me to do something in the gallery.

We were staying at the Mike Steiner Artist Hotel. And we worked out together more and more details about how to do the actions, and I said I want to have it filmed. We tried cameramen in Germany, cameraman in Switzerland and Austria. No way. They all said no when we explained what we would be doing.

One morning, we had breakfast and somebody came in and Mike Steiner introduced us to Jörg Schmidt-Reitwein, a cameraman.

So we got around this table and had coffee together, explained the action, and he, of course, didn't say, "Oh yes I will do that." No, no. But he said, "Okay, let me think about it."

He was thinking about it, and then he said, "Okay, I will do it, I need a camera, I need a car and a driver. Because I will film from inside the car, I will not leave the car whatsoever." And Mike said, "Okay."

So Mike started out, rented a VW bus, drove the bus, he got the camera and then he got Wilma Kottusch involved as the director, though she was more the editor. I was my own director because they followed me while I was on foot. They were in the car and they filmed the action from the car. They didn't believe I'd make it, except when I entered the house of the Turkish family, then they left the car and were inside the house now, and they made a few shots when I entered the apartment with the people and when I changed the painting. That was the only moment they left the car. Then they disappeared while I was waiting for the consequences.

I knew it was on 16mm film and only partly recorded. So I asked Mike Steiner for a copy. Mike said, "I don't have it."

Then we go to Wilma Kottusch and said, "I want to have a copy of this film."

She said, "I don't have it."

She was in the car with the film, she had the film, but now she said she doesn't have it. I'm pretty sure she wanted to hide it, to secure it out of pure speculation that it would later be worth something.

Later on, she went with another cameraman back into the Neue Nationalgalerie and they took shots of the escape route: the subjective shot of the route through the big hall, down the stairs, down to the end there. And then the assistant director of the gallery was very pissed. He approached them, "There is no way you film here." Later on she copied this into the film, because that's like her signature. She also talks to a man, you hear her voice in the tape.

Now I was invited to the Tenth Biennale in Paris, which is extremely prestigious. You see the list of artists included. I was invited solo because of the Berlin "lifting" as it became known, our action. And Georges Boudaille, the director of the Biennale, had approached me and said, "Well, I want to show that film. And if you have photographs." And I thought . . . I didn't say that I *don't* have the film. I go to Mike Steiner and I said, "This is your unique chance to present the film just one year after, now in 1977. And I need either a copy of the film or I need a video."

And he said, "I cannot promise. When is the Biennale?"

I said, "There's still months of time."

He came just in time to Paris, with the video, too, and negatives, stills from the 16mm frames. And we showed it. And it was all right. We showed it, everybody was happy.

I paid him about 350 Deutschmarks (around $800 in today's money). I got some money for expenses from the others. I gave him the 350 to compensate for the material.

Kottusch had stored the film at a film lab in Berlin. The film lab also had editing facilities. So it was there, deposited there. There they had made a U-matic video [a format developed in 1971 and used widely in broadcast television at the time]. I have the original.

They had made the film, from the 16mm film to video format. And they also made single frames from the 16mm film that Mike Steiner brought to Paris. And I paid them, I compensated them.

They both looked at the film, but Mike only got this video version, from which he also made a secondary video transfer for himself for his video gallery. Later on, I worked on that copy. I put the sound on it, and I put many images from the press on it.

Kottusch had never contacted me, and she kept saying to Mike Steiner, "I don't have the film, I don't have the film," which suggests very bad intention. I have one film. Then in 1998, there was quite an incredible, important exhibition in Berlin in Martin-Gropius-Bau called *Deutschlandbilder: Kunst aus einem geteilten Land* exhibition, ["German Images" ran from September 7, 1997, to January 11, 1998, and served as the central event of the Forty-Seventh Berliner Festwochen, showcasing a comprehensive review of art from East and West Germany during the Cold War.] Amazing, beautiful exhibition. Amazing. And the curator was Dr. Eckhart Gillen.

Gillen approached me and said, "I want to build a booth—a black box—and we screen that film inside. I think that's the right idea."

So we did.

I made again a copy for the screening on video—I love video—and during the show Wilma Kottusch appeared, approached Eckhart Gillen, and said, "You have to close the show, you have no rights to screen this film." In 1998! So we're talking about 1976, then I showed it in 1977, I screened it once for the Biennale in Paris, and in 1998, that was only the second time. Then they did close it, and there was correspondence again with a lawyer and Kottusch and me, et cetera.

That was the first mean interference on her part. She claims all the rights to the film, not having given me the copy, not having given me access to it, not having given me the chance to edit with her on it.

I sent a registered letter to Mrs. Kottusch in 1998. I explained the whole thing and also expressed my dislike of her attitude. And this is a registered letter. It came back. She refused to read it. And I explained very well how I'm relying on the video, and that is in German. I was very polite. She refused.

Mike Steiner passed away [in 1999]. He gave his whole video collection to the Stiftung Preußischer Kulturbesitz (Prussian Cultural Heritage Foundation). In 2011–2012, the Hamburger Bahnhof had made a show from the whole collection [called *Live to Tape*]. And for that show they again created a black box in which to screen that film—his version, not my version, his version. The initial version without me having worked on it and without my artistic review.

Then again Kottusch appeared and this time very aggressive. They had to shut it down. There were several lawyers involved.

And then this thing became really big. Hamburger Banhof have their own legal department. They got involved, and she became worse and worse and worse. I had written a long letter explaining the whole thing, also telling that I tried on several occasions to try to contact her, to make a deal with her and to get a copy of the film, and she always flat-out refused. At that point it had been nearly forty years!

The idea behind this is that she of course is aware that Marina is rich and famous. And she thinks that since Marina has something to do with it then Marina is selling the video. Which is not true. Kottusch was asking for one million. I never made money with that film.

If you wanted to get to this video in America, it's on loan or for sale, you go through Electronic Art Intermix [EAI, a nonprofit founded in 1971 by art dealer Howard Wise]. This is the biggest art video distributor. I contacted Electronic Arts Intermix, asked them to take it out of distribution. I have contacted my video distributor in Amsterdam, to take it out of distribution and catalog. They have done so.

I did make some big prints from some negative stills from the video. They were sold at Artissima [a contemporary art fair] in Turin to Castello di Rivoli Museo d'Arte Contemporanea [Turin's leading contemporary art museum]. It's a great museum, a great collection, and it's completely legitimate. Only I gave them the video as a gift. They didn't buy it. They got the video as a gift because they bought some prints I made from the stills.

I paid Mike Steiner for his part. The thing is that Kottusch did not collaborate. She never gave me access to the film to have a say in the creative side. I only worked on a copy of it. She did not direct it because she was in the car, in the back seat, while someone else was filming. I was the director as well as the focus of the action. I did the action and I directed myself. I had written the concept and the script for it. So that is all bullshit, what she was saying.

THE KICKER

Sometime later, the painting was stolen. Well, the Neue Nationalgalerie had decided to bring the whole German Romantic painting collection to Schloss Charlottenburg. It's a beautiful chateau and a more appropriate place. And then, in 1989 two men entered the museum chateau with the painting collection, one in a wheelchair and the other one pushed the wheelchair. And they went straight to this painting. They grabbed it, tore it from the wall. There was a guard. They turned around and hit the guard with a heavy frame mount and the guard was knocked out, and they ran away with it.

And then the interesting thing is that sometime later, a short, short time later, in a German newspaper there was a little advertisement: A Japanese industrialist looks for Spitzweg paintings. Just shortly after, which is strange.

I think it goes to the Russian mafia. The drugs and arms dealers. And they use them as down payment or something, that's usually what they do. But it's interesting that in Japan there is a law: If you can prove that you have a stolen artefact or work of art for more than two years, then it is legally yours. [This is a common misinterpretation of Japanese statutes of limitations on stolen property and the "good faith acquisition" provision of the Civil Code, but it is so commonly misunderstood that even criminals sometimes act with the assumption that stolen art can be "cooled off" in Japan and then shopped around after two years without fear of imprisonment.]

Well, tonight we will put my version on the screen, and we will film it from the monitor, so that you see just the edge of the monitor. In this way, we'll reshoot it from the monitor and that means I'm just "stealing" whatever is on the screen? And before that I will sit in front of the screen and make just a declaration, like "My name is Ulay and I hereby declare the video recording to be my own work." I'll make an edition of it.

The first eleven images provided are stills from the video of the action. They form something of a storyboard of the action when viewed

Images

in sequence, from Ulay removing the painting from the wall, tucking it under his arm, fleeing the museum, driving away in his and Marina's van, driving across town, sprinting through the snow, then hanging the painting on an immigrant family's wall.

The remaining images were gathered and kept by Ulay in his archive. These include the cover of the Steiner Gallery's catalog about the action and a collage of relics of it: Ulay's outline of the action, a map of his planned route from the museum to the apartment, and press clippings that he kept after the event. All are reproduced here courtesy of the Ulay Foundation.

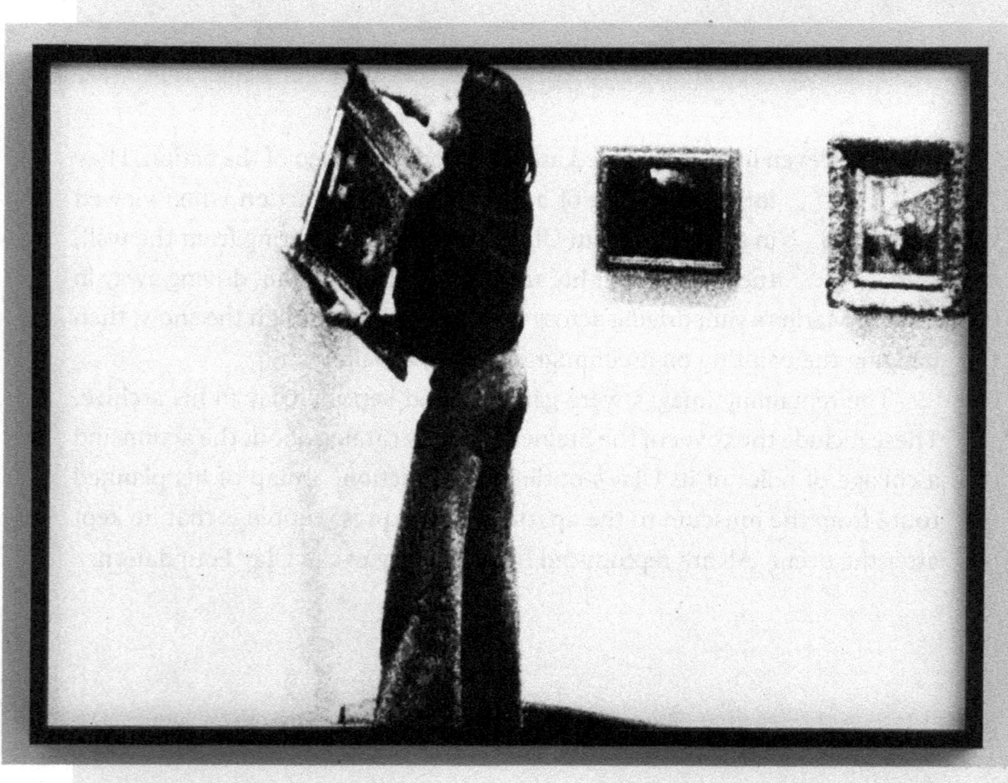

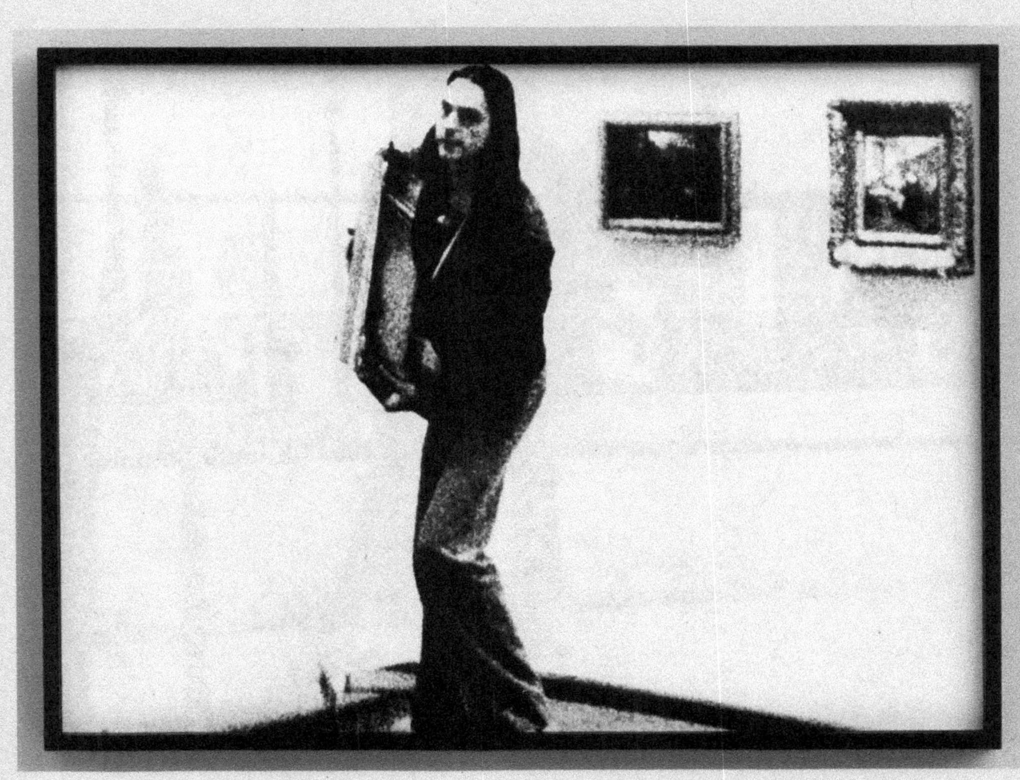

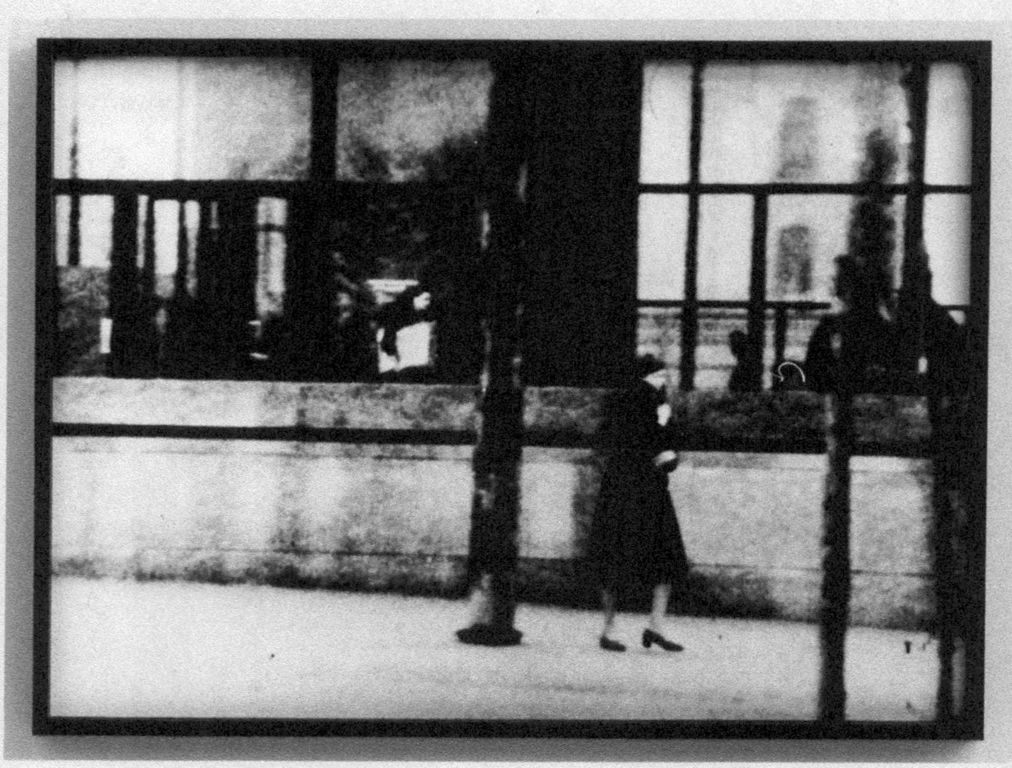

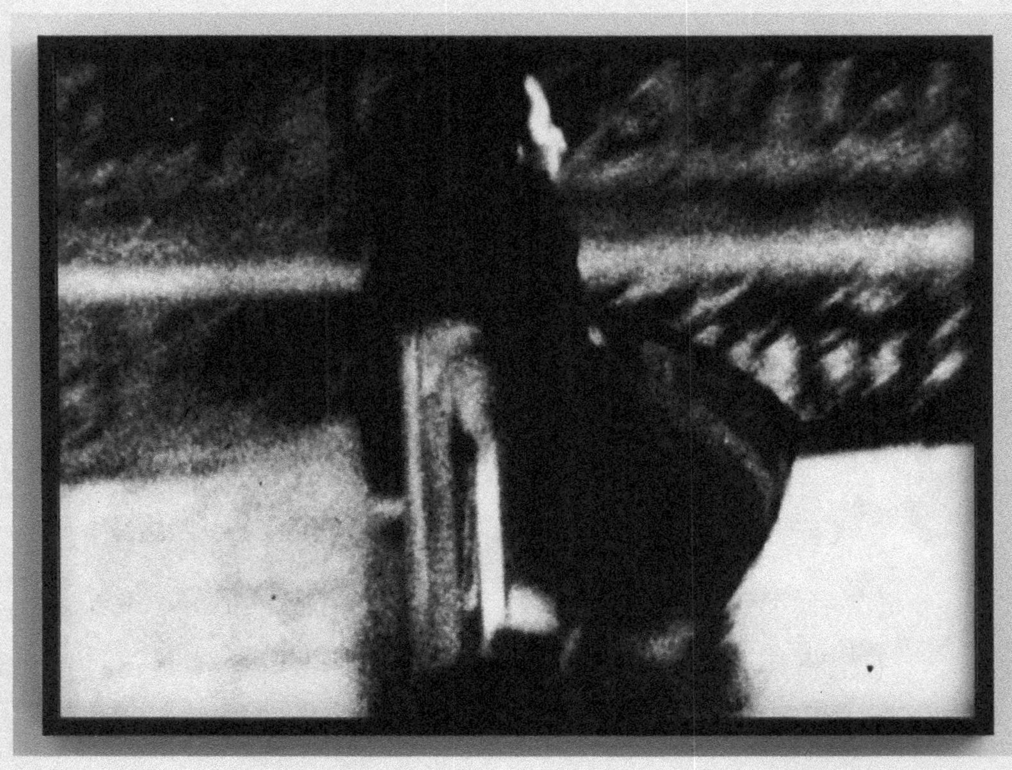

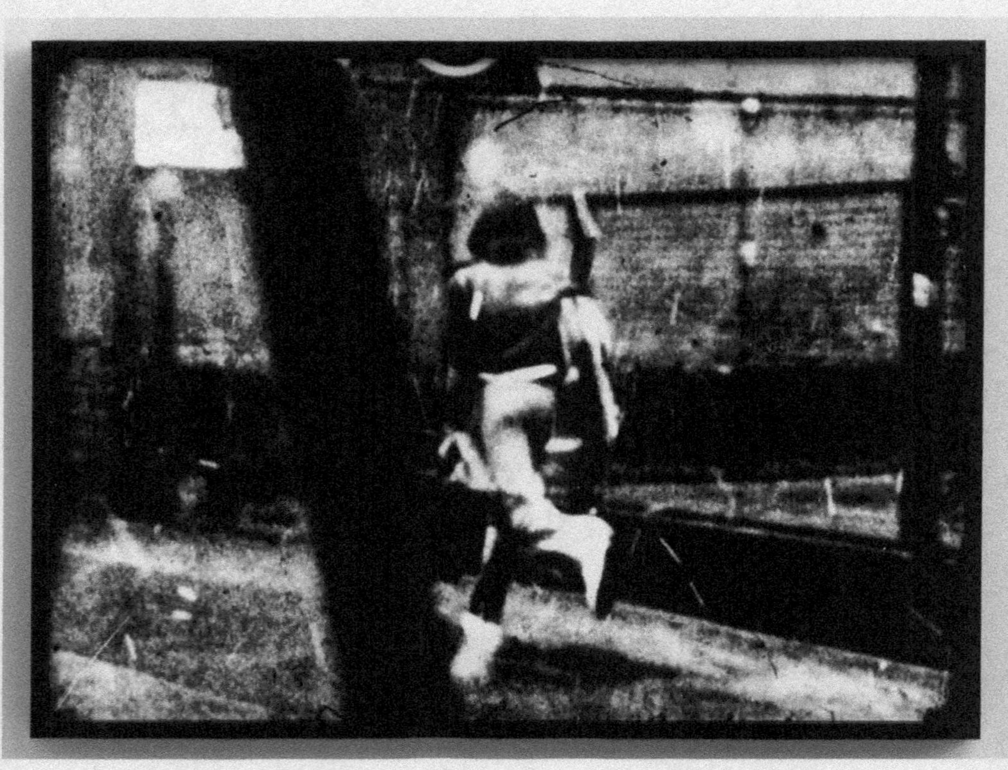

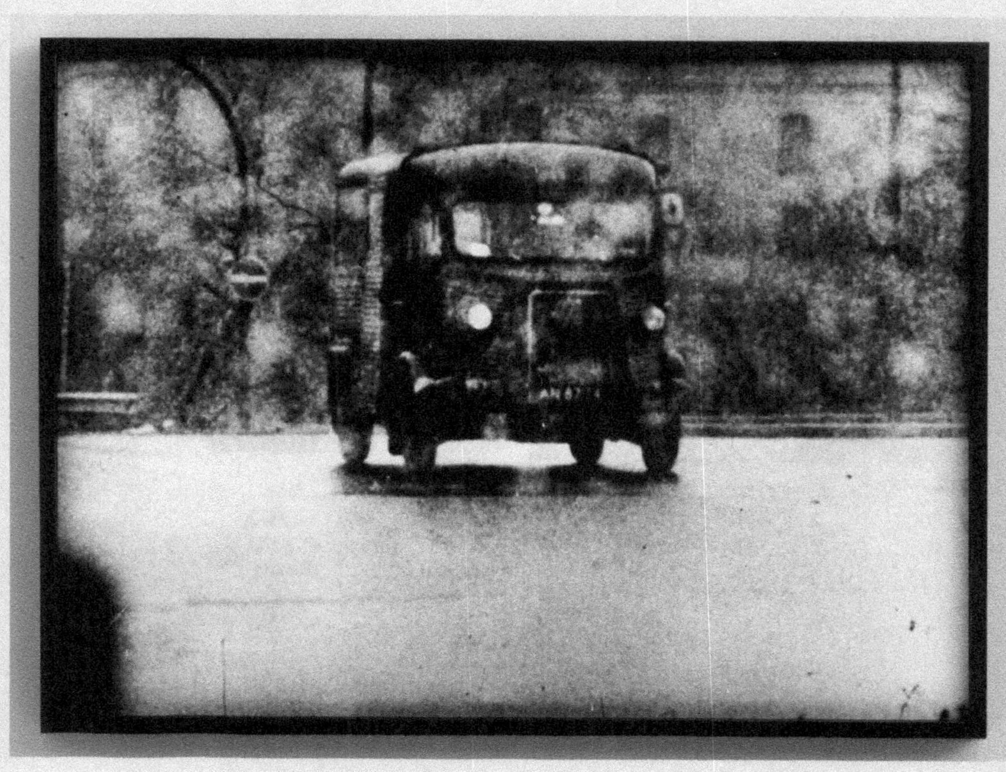

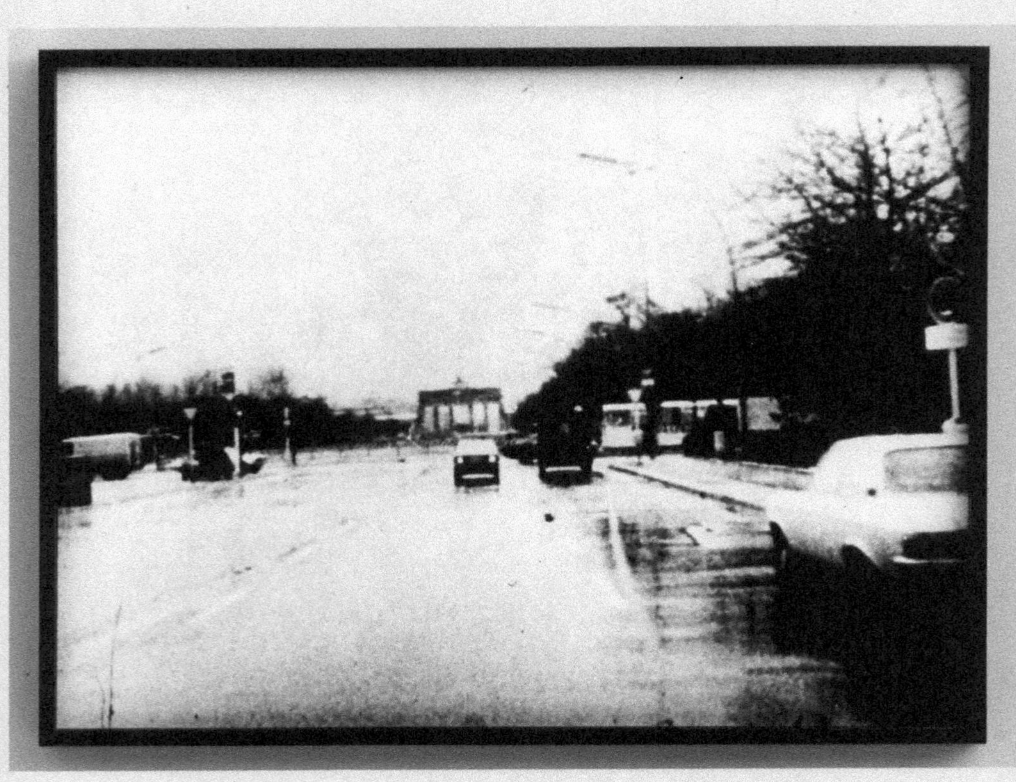

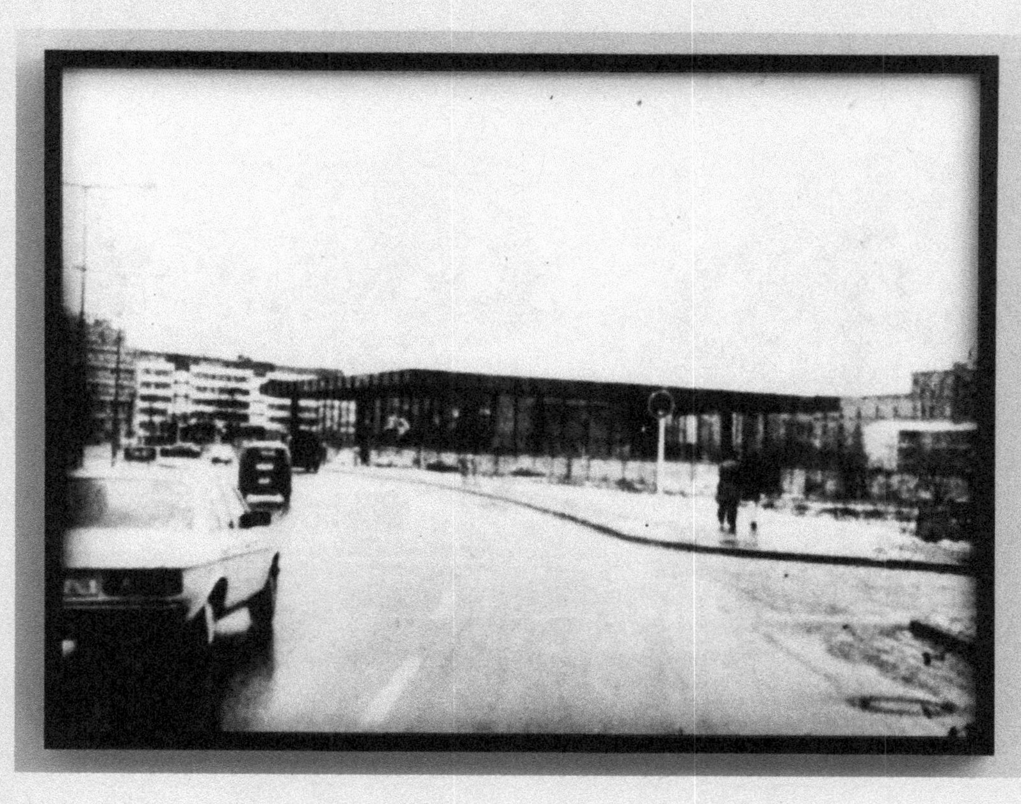

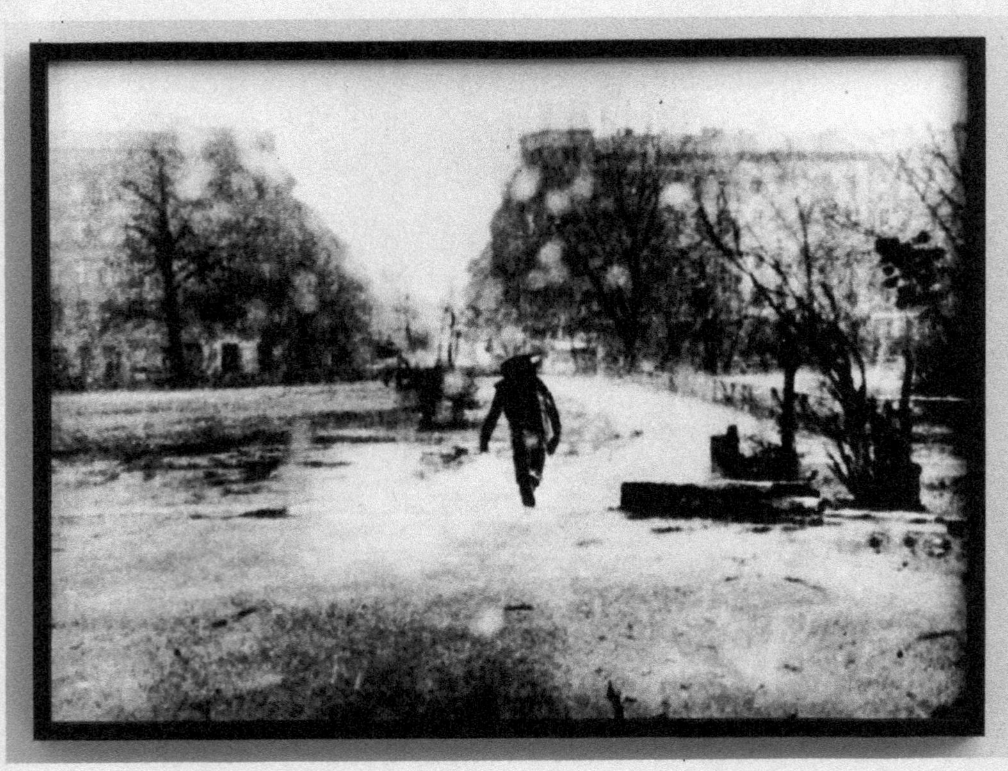

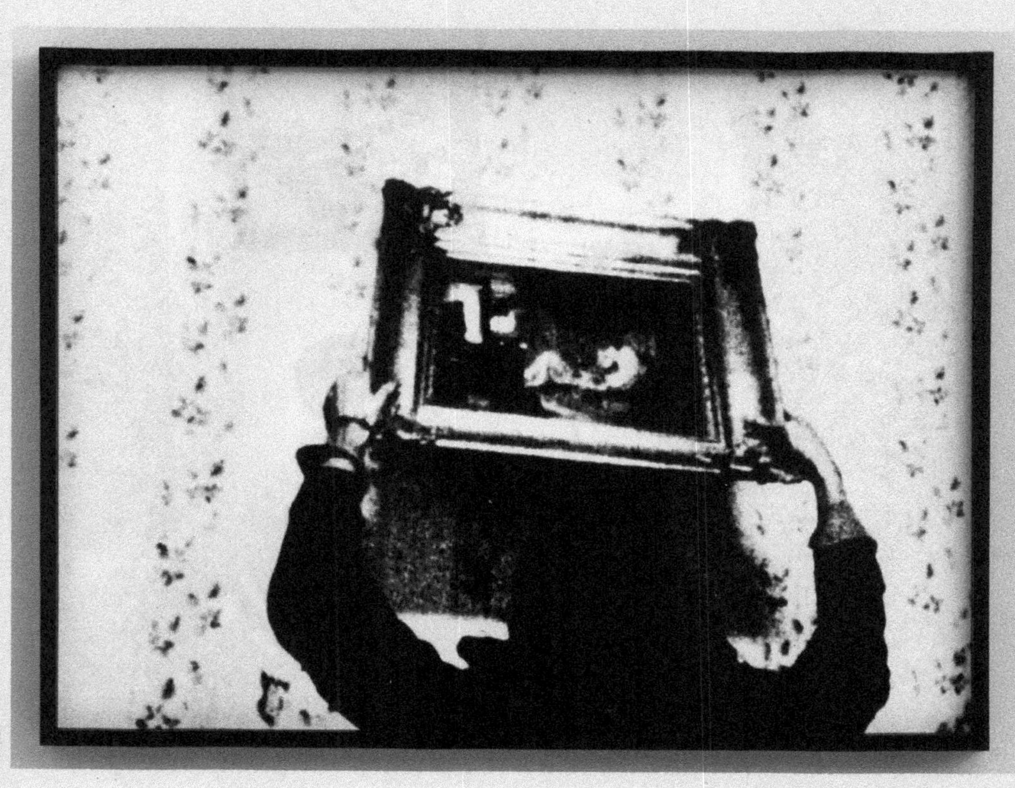

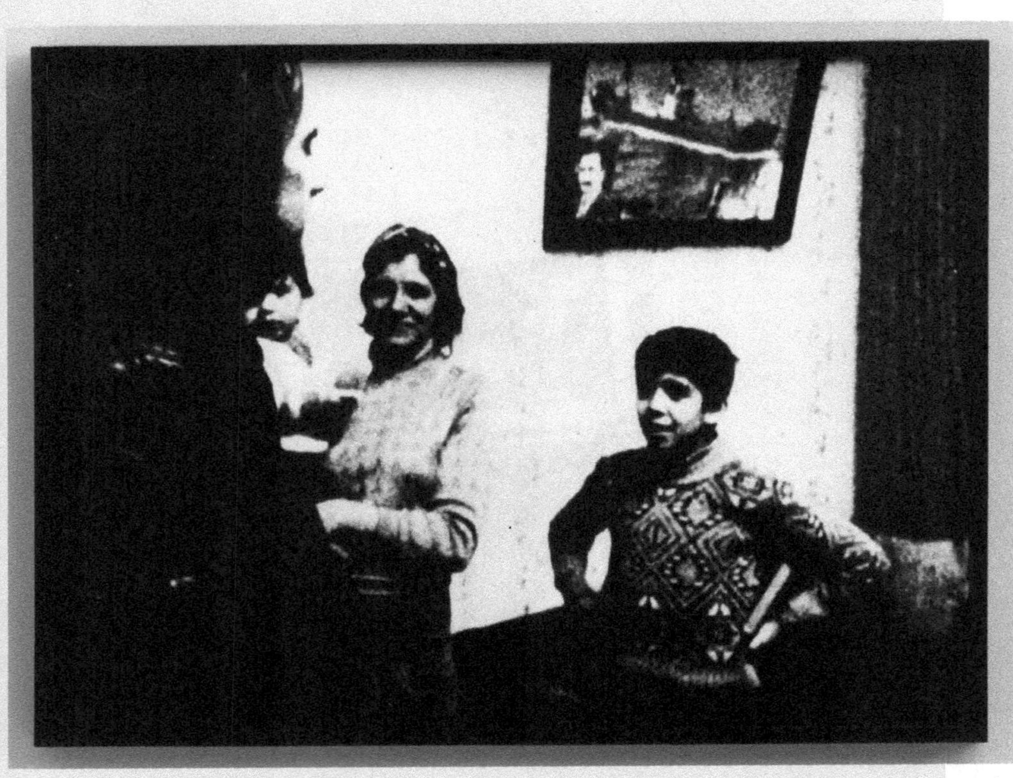

U L A Y
IRRITATION

STUDIOGALERIE STEINER

ULAY

...DA IST EINE "KRIMINELLE" BERÜHRUNG IN DER KUNST

IRRITATION

Dokument einer Aktion

Ein Film von Wilma Kottusch und Mike Steiner
Kamera: Jörg-Schmidt Reitwein

b/w 20 Min. Gefilmt anläßlich der Aktion:
  DA IST EINE KRIMINELLE BERÜHRUNG IN DER KUNST
an den Originalplätzen.

Alle Fotografien entstammen dem Film. Vertrieb
WMK-Produktion Berlin.

BESCHREIBUNG DER AKTION

1. Hänge vor den Haupteingang der Hochschule der
   bildenden Künste eine Fotofahne (200x250 cm),
   Motiv: Reproduktion des Spitzweg Gemäldes
   "Der arme Poet"
2. fahre mit eigenem Wagen zur Neuen Nationalgalerie,
3. parke Wagen an der Rückseite der Neuen
   Nationalgalerie,
4. gehe in die Neue Nationalgalerie,
5. entferne aus der Neuen Nationalgalerie das
   Gemälde "der arme Poet" von Carl Spitzweg
6. laufe mit dem Gemälde aus der Neuen Nationalgaleri
   zu meinem Wagen,
7. fahre Richtung Berlin-Kreuzberg,
8. parke Wagen in Berlin-Kreuzberg,
9. laufe mit Gemälde weiter zum Künstlerhaus
   Bethanien,
10. hänge vor den Haupteingang des Künstlerhaus
    Bethanien eine Farbreproduktion des Spitzweg
    Gemäldes,
11. laufe weiter mit dem Gemälde in die Muskauer-
    strasse,
12. betrete ein Haus für türkische Gastarbeiter,
13. gehe in die Wohnung einer Gastarbeiterfamilie,
14. hänge das Gemälde "der arme Poet" an die Wand.

   Berlin, 12.12.1976

ZUM GEMÄLDE "Der arme Poet" (1839)

Carl Spitzweg, geboren 1808 in München, gestorben
Spitzwegs " der arme Poet " existiert in drei
Versionen, wovon sich eine in der Neuen Nationalgalerie, Berlin, die zweite in der Münchener Pinak
und die dritte in einer privaten Sammlung befinden

Einer seiner größten Verehrer, der von ihm 50 Bild
besaß, plante den Bau eines Mammut-Spitzweg-Museum
in Linz (Österreich): Adolf Hitler.

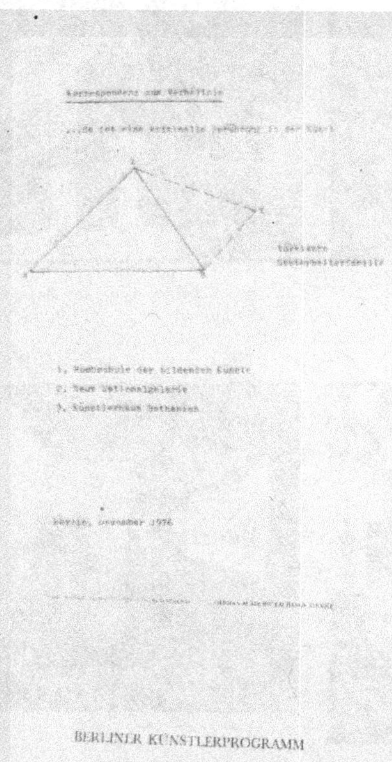

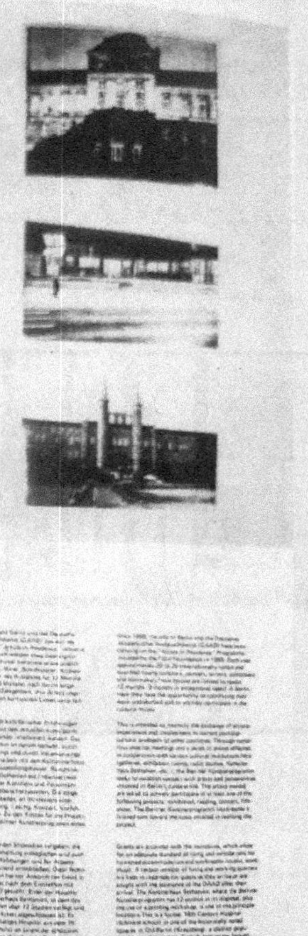

BERLINER KÜNSTLERPROGRAMM

ARTISTS IN BERLIN PROGRAMME

Informationen und Hinweise   Information and Remarks

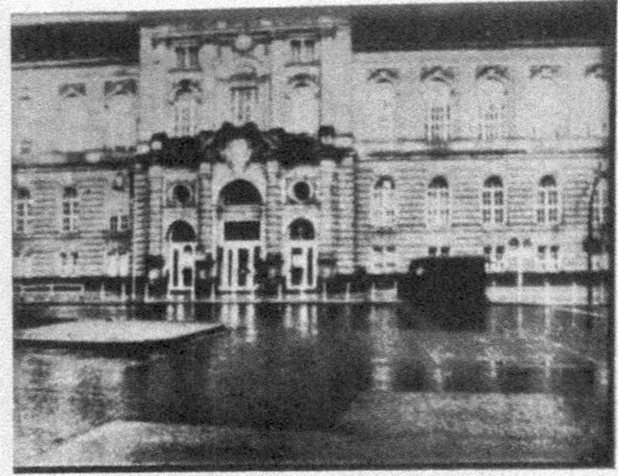

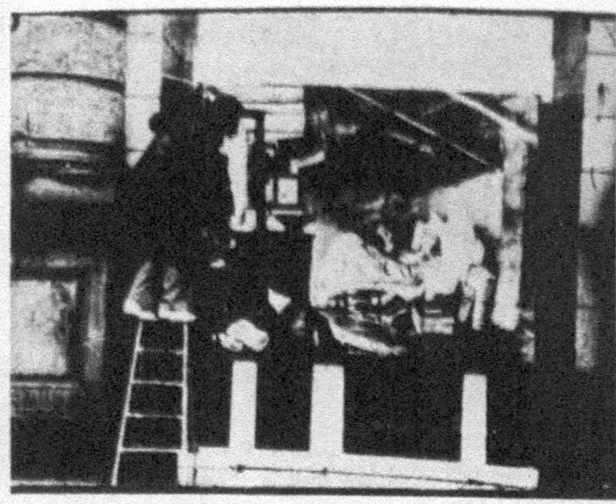

1. Beginn der Aktion, der Haupteingang der
   Hochschule der Künste wird verhängt, ein
   betreten des Gebäudes ist nicht mehr möglich.

2. Ausgerollte Reproduktion des "armen Poeten".
   12.51 Uhr

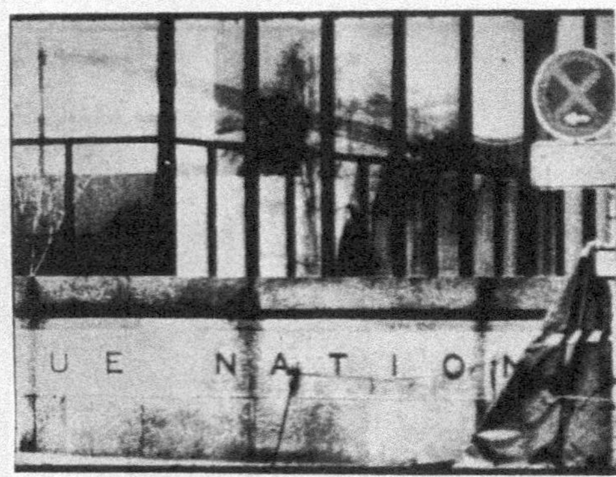

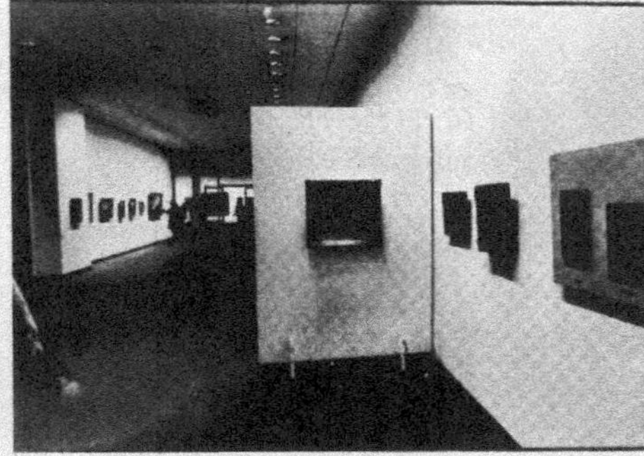

5. Beim Eintreten in die Neue Nationalgalerie.
   1.07 Uhr

6. Biedermeier-Saal mit Spitzweg Gemälde in der
   Neuen Nationalgalerie.

8. Verlassen der Neuen Nationalgalerie mit dem
   Gemälde.

9. Fahrt in Richtung Kreuzberg mit eigenem
   Fahrzeug.

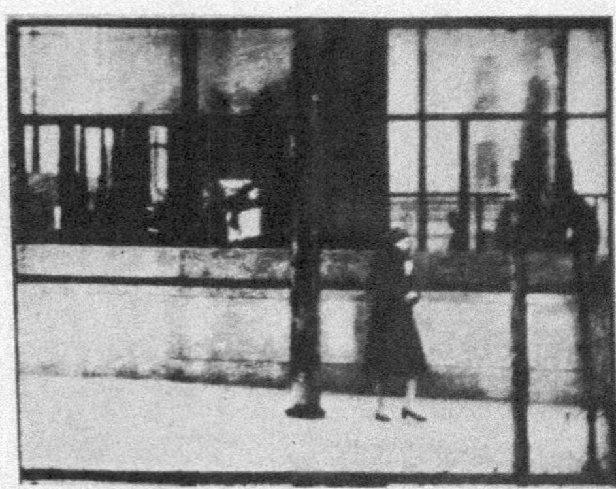

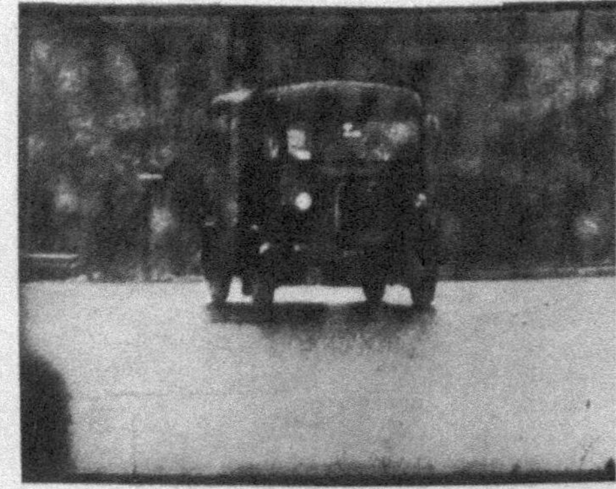

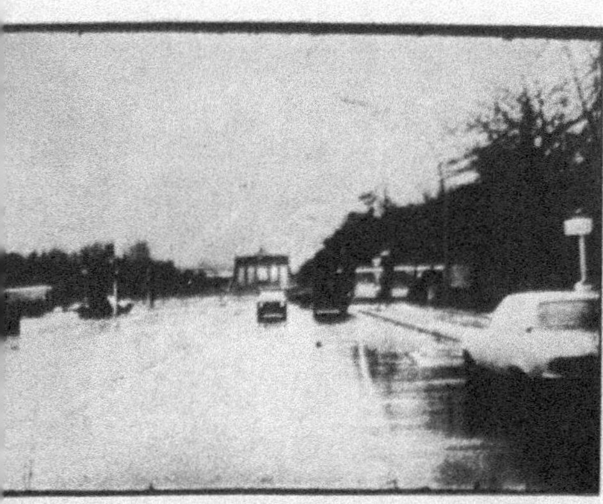 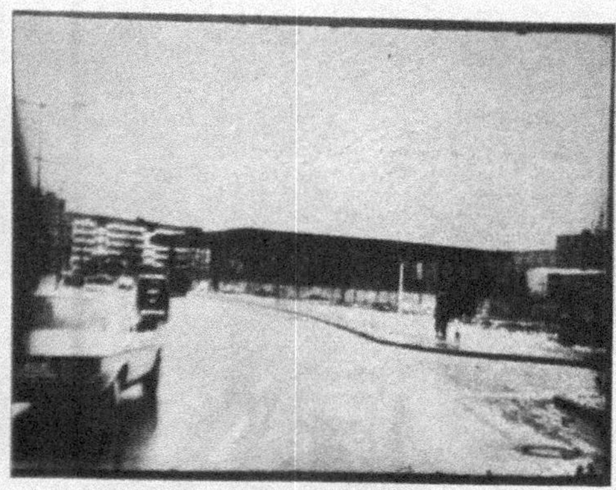

. Fahrt mit dem Auto in Richtung Neue Nationalgalerie.

4. Ankunft vor der Neuen Nationalgalerie 12.59 Uhr

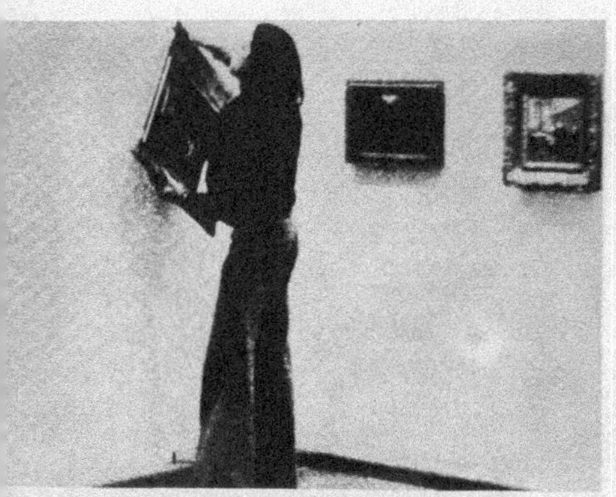 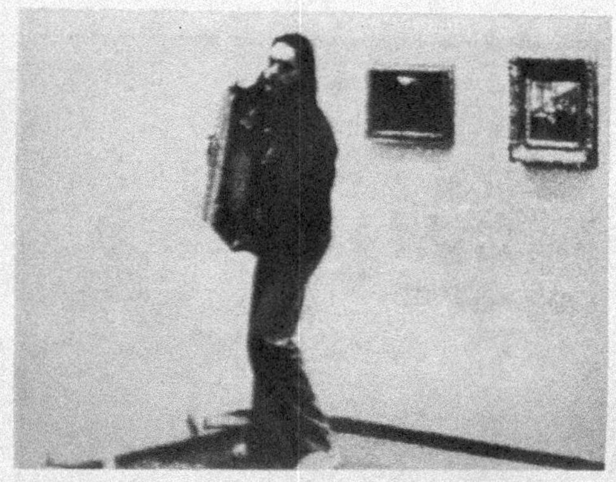

. Abhängung und Auslösen der Alarmanlage
1.11 Uhr.

).Verlassen des Fahrzeuges.   1.17 Uhr

12.Lauf zum Künstlerhaus Bethanien.

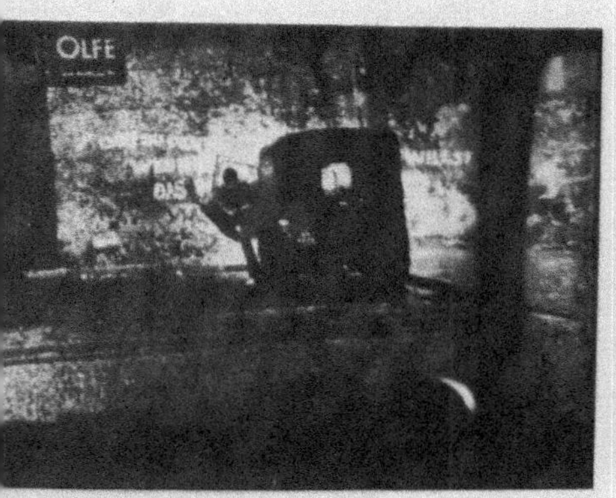 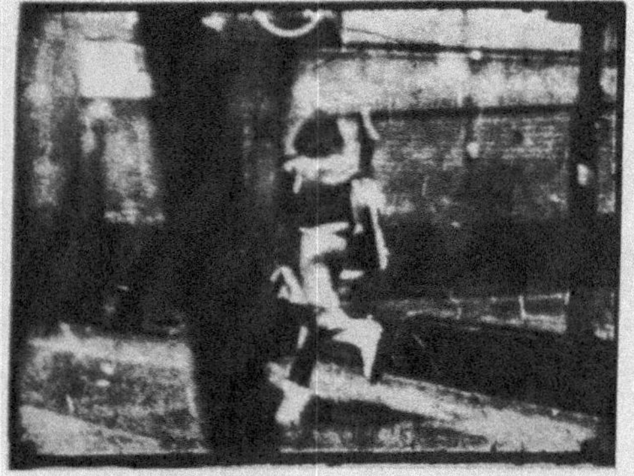

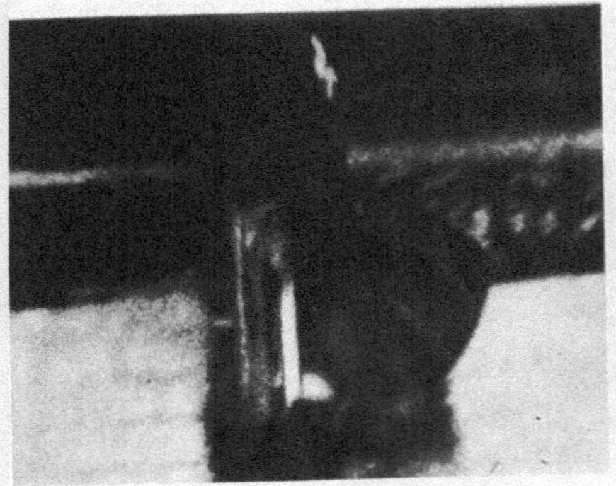

13.Ankunft am Künstlerhaus Bethanien

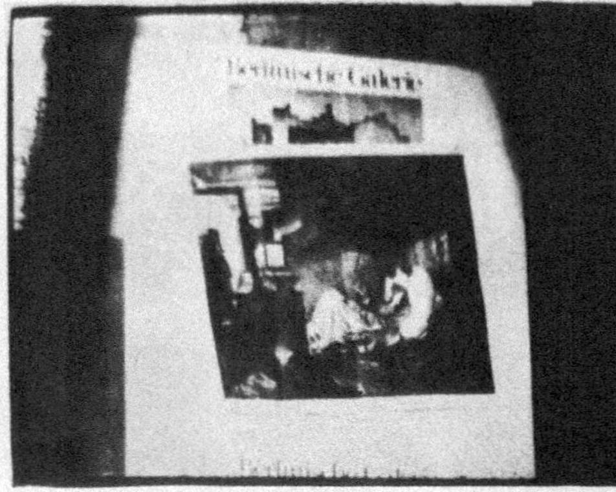

14.Anbringung des Plakates mit der Reproduktion.
   1.20 Uhr

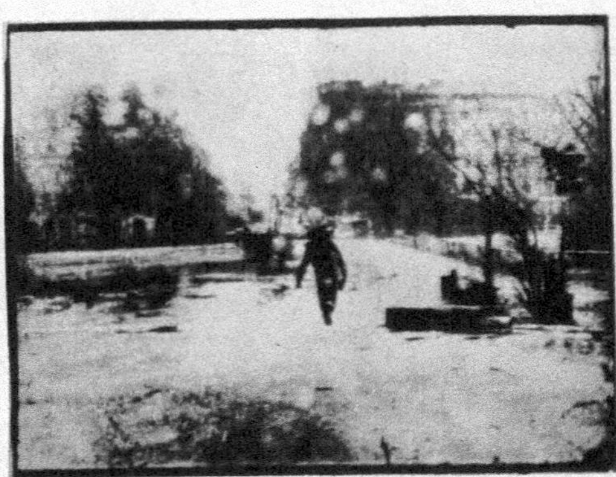

15.Lauf in Richtung Muskauer Strasse, welche sich
   gegenüber dem Künstlerhaus Bethanien befindet.

17.Abhängung des "Engelbildes"

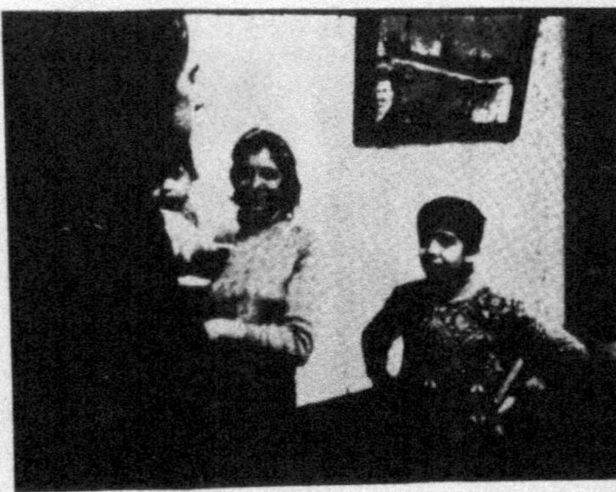

16.Ankunft mit dem "armen Poeten" in der
   Gastarbeiterfamilie.   1.22 Uhr

18.Ende der Aktion: Ein Kitschprodukt wird gegen
   das andere Kitschprodukt ausgetauscht. 1.23 Uhr

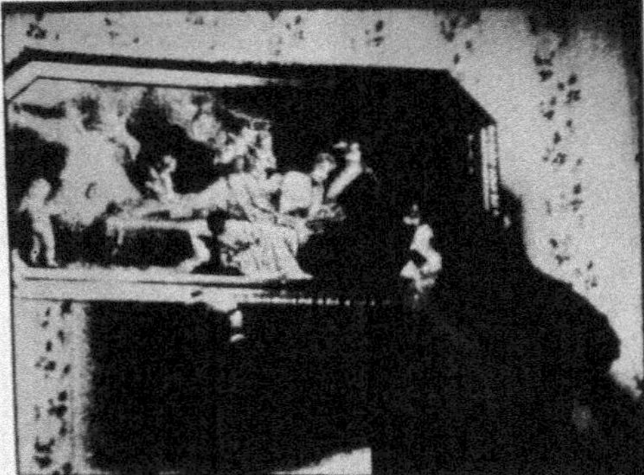

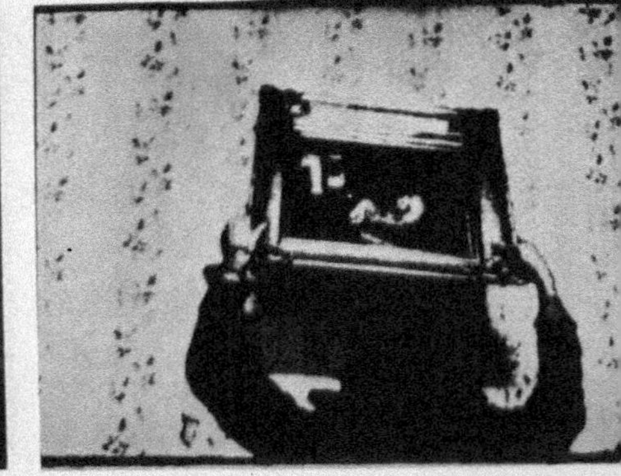

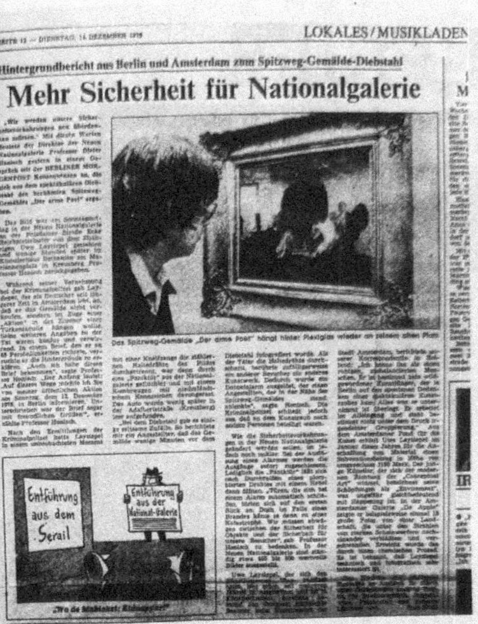

Hintergrundbericht aus Berlin und Amsterdam zum Spitzweg-Gemälde-Diebstahl

Mehr Sicherheit für Nationalgalerie

Das Spitzweg-Gemälde „Der arme Poet" hängt hinter Plexiglas wieder an seinem alten Platz

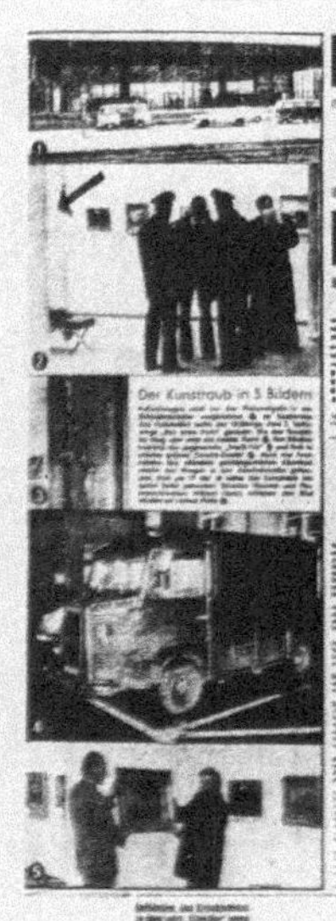

Berlins Museen sind sehr sicher - aber leider nur nachts...

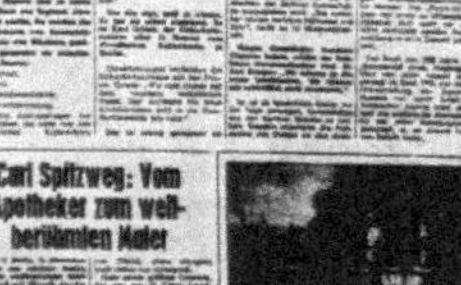

Carl Spitzweg: Vom Apotheker zum weltberühmten Maler

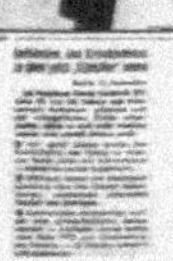

Warum Spitzweg seinen armen Poeten gleich dreimal malte

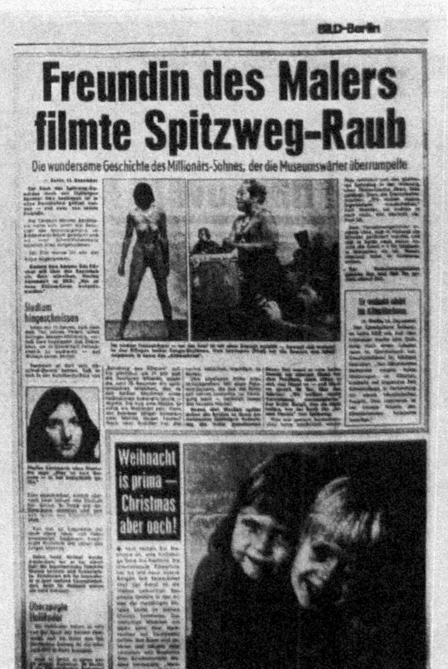

Freundin des Malers filmte Spitzweg-Raub

Die wundersame Geschichte des Millionärs-Sohnes, der die Museumswärter überrumpelte

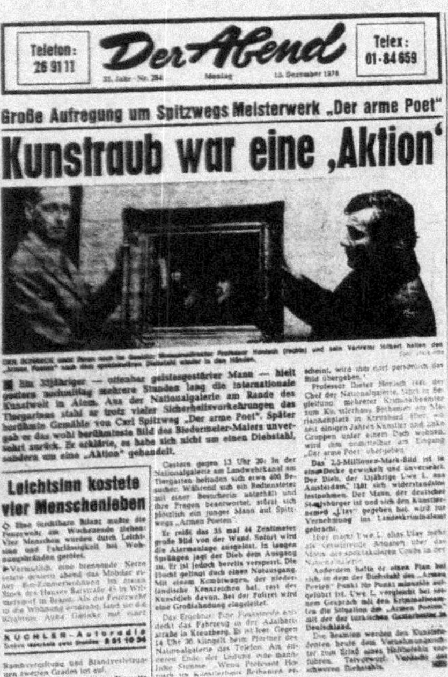

Große Aufregung um Spitzwegs Meisterwerk „Der arme Poet"

Kunstraub war eine ,Aktion'

Leichtsinn kostete vier Menschenleben

Der arme Poet sitzt jetzt unter Plexiglas

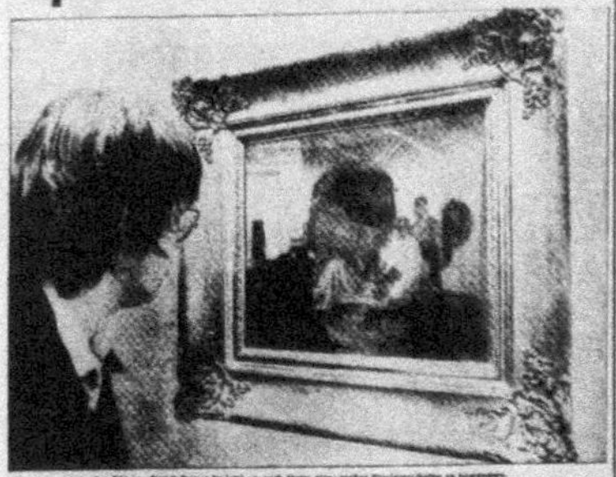

Verstärkte Sicherung für das Spitzweg-Gemälde, in dem sich jetzt die Besucher spiegeln

Berlin: Linksradikaler raubte unser schönstes Bild

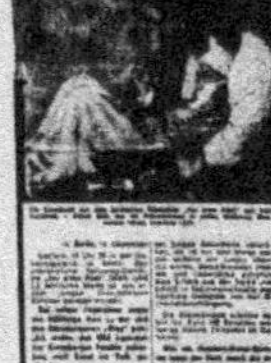

t seinem Bilderdiebstahl wollte der Kunststudent „Ulay" gegen die Lebensbedingungen der Gastarbeiter protestieren

„Armer Poet" sollte Türken-Wohnung zieren

arl Spitzwegs „Der arme Poet" soll nach dem Diebstahl aus der Neuen Nationalgalerie in der Wohnung einer kischen Gastarbeiterfamilie im Kreuzer Viertel Adalbertstraße/Naunynaße hängen. Das ging aus einem „Aktionsplan" des gestern festgenommenen ländischen Gemäldediebes Uwe Laysio, Künstlername „Ulay" hervor. Der dent, der in Berlin freiberuflich als nstmaler arbeitet, wollte von dem rühmten Biedermeier-Bild Reproduktionen anfertigen und als Fototransparente im Format 250×200 Zentimeter der Fassade der Hochschule für nste in der Hardenbergstraße und Künstlerhauses Bethanien in Kreuzg anbringen.

Der aus Amsterdam stammende Student mit der deutschen Staatsbürgerschaft lebt unter Künstlern in dem frühen Krankenhaus Bethanien, das zeitweise auch von linken und anarchistischen Gruppierungen als Domizil besetzt worden ist.

Dort übergab „Ulay" gestern nachmittag das Spitzweg-Gemälde.

Es war in eine Decke eingewickelt und unversehrt. Wie die Polizei nach einer Vernehmung am Abend mitteilte, gab der Student eine verwirrende Darstellung der Vorgänge. Vermutlich sei er „geistesgestört", hieß es in einem Bericht der Nachrichtenagentur Associated Press. Mit dem Diebstahl habe er nach seinen Angaben gegen den internationalen Kunstbetrieb und die Lebensdingungen der Türken in der Bundesrepublik einschließlich West-Berlins protestieren wollen.

Der Festgenommene soll heute dem Vernehmungsrichter wegen schweren Diebstahls vorgeführt werden. In der Vernehmung hatte er ausgesagt, ihm habe niemand geholfen oder Ratschläge geben. Auf die Idee zu seiner Aktion ist er im vergangenen Oktober bei einem ersten Besuch in Berlin gekommen. In dem Zeitplan, den die Polizei bei ihm fand, hatte er vorgesehen, nach dem Diebstahl mit dem Wagen zum nahegelegenen U-Bahnhof Möckernbrücke zu fahren und in die Untergrundbahn zu steigen. Auf dem Bahnhof Kottbusser Tor wollte er den Zug verlassen und die ihm bekannte türkische Familie aufsuchen. In einer Erklärung, die er zuvor verfaßt hatte, heißt es unter anderem:

„Zum Anlaß zu dieser Aktion kam ich seitens meines Aufenthalts in Berlin, im Oktober 1976.

Dies ist der Grund, warum diese Aktion in Berlin stattfindet und konzeptgemäß eine Authenzität festgelegt ist. Die generelle Motivation trifft aber auf den gesamten internationalen Kunstbetrieb zu.

Ich markiere drei maßgebende Kulturinstitute, zwischen diesen bewege ich mich mit einer Reproduktion des Gemäldes von Carl Spitzweg „Der arme Poet". Das Original befindet sich in der Neuen Nationalgalerie, das dritte der markierten Institute.

Das genannte Gemälde ist als Modell im Rahmen der Aktion zu sehen. Gemäß meiner Kritik versetze ich das Gemälde aus dem Kontext der neuen Nationalgalerie (Museum Funktion) in die Situation, die Wohnung einer türkischen Gastarbeiterfamilie.

Der Aspekt „Kriminelle Berührung" ist nicht in der Form der Aktion zu sehen, sondern in den Punkten der mittels der Aktion aufgerufenen Kritik im Bereich der Kulturinstitute, deren Aufgabe und Funktion, als auch im Sinne einer Kunstkritik.

Für die Richtigkeit und Schwergewicht dieser Kritik findet innerhalb dieser Aktion eine Grenzübertretung statt, ich trete als Künstler aus der Protektion des Kunst/Künstlerbereichs in einen offenen Lebensbereich Ulay"

Die Neue Nationalgalerie der Staatlichen Museen Preußischer Kulturbesitz wurde 1965 bis 1968 erbaut. Schwerpunkte der Gemälde, Skulpturen und Handzeichnungen des 19. und 20. Jahrhunderts sind die deutsche Romantik, der Realismus, Impressionisten, Expressionismus und Kunst der Gegenwart.

L.B.

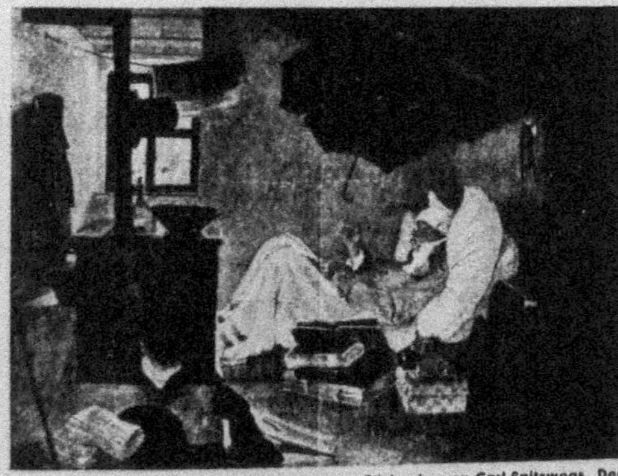

Der Zufall führte Regie: vier Stunden nach der Rückgabe von Carl Spitzwegs „Der arme Poet" war das Gemälde im ZDF-„Hofkonzert" zu sehen.

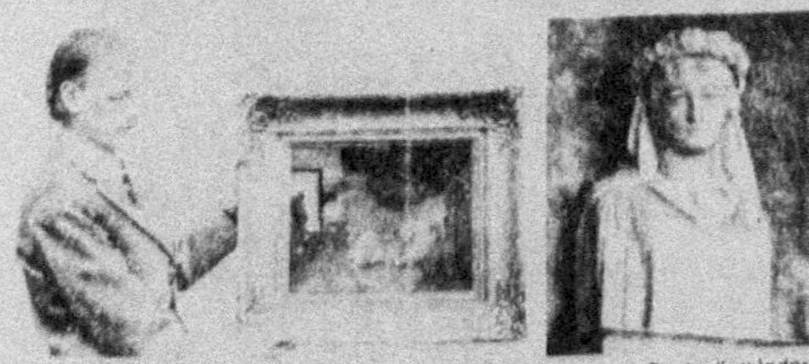

Gestern nachmittag hatte die Museumsleitung den „Armen Poeten" wieder. Rechts: Ähnlich endete 1962 der Diebstahl einer Büste der Königin Luise.

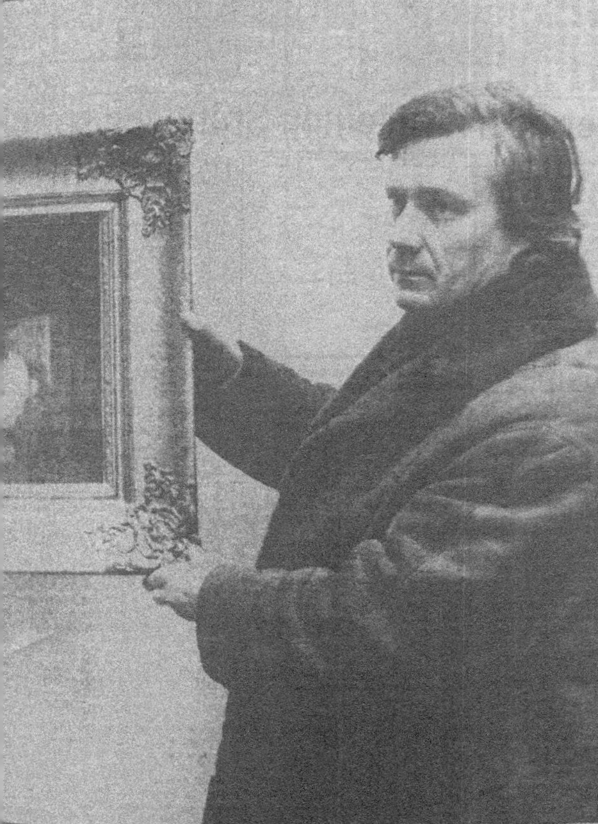

der Schreck im Gesicht. Aber: Das Bild ist unversehrt zurück und kann wieder an seinen Platz kommen.

...ines Films aus der Spitzweg-Zeit

...setze ich das
...Kontext der
...alerie   (Mu-
...die Situation,
... türkischen
... Ich tre-
... der Protek-
...reiches in ei-
...bereich."

**...stahl
...ung**

...er 17 Punkte
..."Ulay" unter
...das Gemälde
... der armu-
...ng der Gast-
...lie Wand."
...te er unter
...000 Meter
... Nähe
...r türkischen
...s."

Punkt 17 heißt kurz und bün-
dig: „Ich wache."

So wollte er im Künstler-
haus Bethanien neben einem
Kunstkalender 1977 mit der Farb-
reproduktion des Spitzweg-Bil-
des auf das warten, was dann
kommen sollte ...

Spitzwegs „Der arme Poet", Öl
auf Leinwand, gemalt 1839 in
München, ist 36,2×44,6 Zentimeter groß. Das Bild ist damit in
der Breite eine Handbreit klei-
ner als diese beiden Seiten dieser Zeitung. Ein kunstvoller
Rahmen läßt dieses Bild an der
Wand allerdings größer erschei-
nen.

Die Nationalgalerie wurde
1968 eröffnet. Es war der erste
Diebstahl in dieser Zeit. Die
Anlagen der Galerie gelten als ...

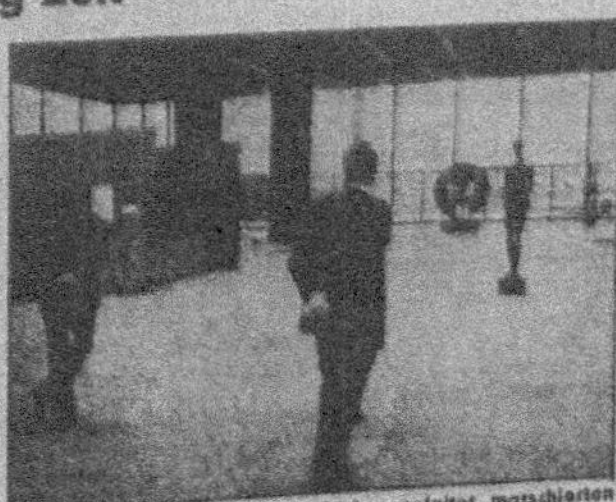

Nervös, die Hände auf dem Rücken gefaltet, marschierten
Mitarbeiter nach dem Raub durchs Erdgeschoß.

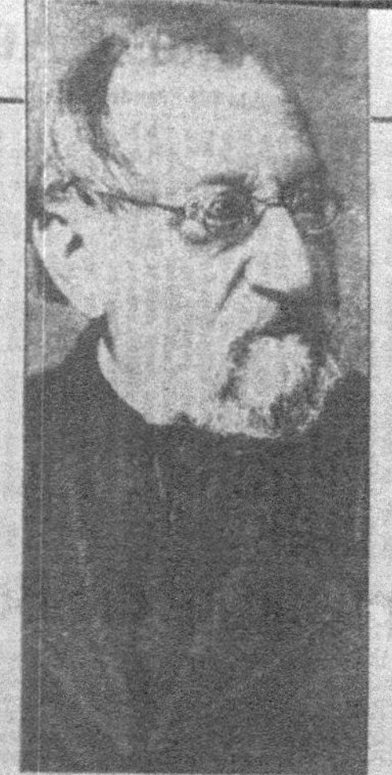

Carl Spitzweg (1808—1885): Er begann als
Apotheker und endete als großer Maler.

Der Maler, der seine Bilder auch auf die Deckel von Zigarrenkisten malte

Berlin, 13. Dezember

77 Jahre alt wurde der Maler und Apotheker Carl Spitzweg. 1885 ist er in seiner Zweizimmer-Wohnung am Münchener Heumarkt gestorben.

Sein Grabmal hat er sich
so vorgestellt:

„Ein Hauben-Puppendeckel
mit Karpaper geschmackvoll
überzogen. Das Ganze möge
die Form einer Hanswur-
sten-Mütze haben. In der
Mitte müßte ein Relief ange-
bracht sein, worauf alle, die
ich in meinem ganzen Leben
gemalt habe, wütend um Ra-
che schreien ..."

Das berühmteste von 1543
Spitzweg-Bildern wurde sein
„Armer Poet". In drei ver-
schiedenen Fassungen hat er
1839 den kleinen Mann mit
dem Regenschirm über dem
Bett gemalt.

Das Bild in der National-
Galerie ist das erste. Poet
Nummer zwei hängt in der
Bayerischen Staatsgemälde-
Sammlung in München. Das
dritte gehört einem Privat-
mann.

Vorbild für den armen
Poeten soll ein Münchener
Dichter namens Entenhuber
gewesen sein.

Spitzwegs Liebe galt schon
früh der Malerei. Aber er
brachte erst sein Studium
der Pharmazie mit der Note
„Ausgezeichnet" zu Ende.

Er kannte viele Länder

Danach widmete er sich
den Farben, der Leinwand
und — den Schmalseiten seiner Zigarren-Kistchen.

Die warf der leidenschaft-
liche Raucher nie weg. Auf
dem Holz entstanden kleine
Landschaften, lebten Leute
in Wohnungen.

Spitzweg war ein vielgerei-
ster Mann. Er kannte Frank-
reich, Italien, den Balkan. Er
sprach Italienisch, Franzö-
sisch und Englisch. Latein
beherrschte er wie seine
Muttersprache.

Sein Leben lang blieb er
Junggeselle. Er hat eine ver-
heiratete Webarstochter ge-
liebt, die sich seinetwegen
scheiden ließ. Aber kurz dar-
auf starb sie. Das hat Spitzweg nie verwunden.

Hühner für den Suppentopf

Dennoch wurde er nicht
zum Hagestolz. Bei seinen
Freunden — zu ihnen gehör-
te auch der Maler Moritz
von Schwind — war er gern
gesehen. Jeden Sonntag stif-
tete er reihum für drei be-
freundete Familien das Huhn
für den Suppentopf.

Die Malerei hat er sich sel-
ber beigebracht. Ein Großteil
seiner Reisen galt dem Studium anderer Maler. Stun-
denlang verweilte der Mann
mit dem roten Haarschopf
und der schweren Silberbril-
le über den dunklen Augen
in Museen.

Neben der Malerei hat er
sich auch als Poet versucht,
als ebenso liebevoller Spötter
wie in seinen Bildern.

Seit 1844 hat er an den
„Fliegenden Blättern" mitge-
arbeitet, hat dort seine leise
Kritik „verkauft".

Bis vor einigen Jahren galt
Spitzweg „nur" als Maler einer kleinen, heilen Bieder-
meier-Welt voller Gemüt-
lichkeit.

Dahinter aber steckte eine
ganze Portion Bitternis, Re-
signation und Kritik. Auch
beim armen Poeten, dem es
in die Stube regnet und der
sein Zimmer nicht heizen
kann ...   Caroline Meikner

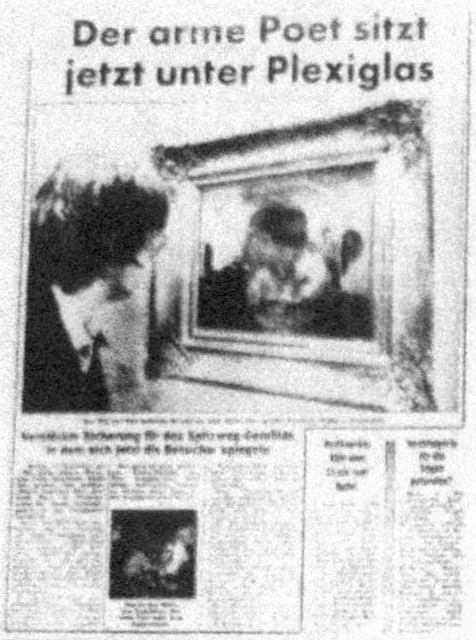

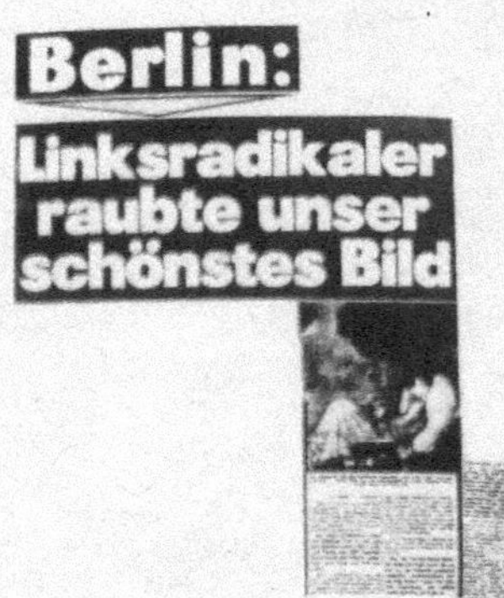

Mit seinem Bilderdiebstahl wollte der Kunststudent „Ulay" gegen die Lebensbedingungen der Gastarbeiter protestieren

„Armer Poet" sollte Türken-Wohnung zieren

Carl Spitzwegs „Der arme Poet" sollte nach dem Diebstahl aus der Neuen Nationalgalerie in der Wohnung einer türkischen Gastarbeiterfamilie im Kreuzberger Viertel Adalbertstraße Naunynstraße hängen. Das ging aus einem „Aktionsplan" des gestern festgenommenen holländischen Gemäldediebes Uwe Layssen, Künstlername „Ulay" hervor. Der Student, der in Berlin freiberuflich als Kunstmaler arbeitet, wollte von dem berühmten Biedermeier-Bild Reproduktionen anfertigen und als Fototransparente im Format 250×200 Zentimeter an der Fassade der Hochschule für Künste in der Hardenbergstraße und des Künstlerhauses Bethanien in Kreuzberg anbringen.

Der aus Amsterdam stammende Student mit der deutschen Staatsbürgerschaft lebt unter Künstlern in dem früheren Krankenhaus Bethanien, das zeitweise auch von Linken und anarchistischen Gruppierungen als Domizil benutzt worden ist.

Dort übergab „Ulay" gestern nachmittag das Spitzweg-Gemälde. Es war in eine Decke eingewickelt und unversehrt. Wie die Polizei nach einer Vernehmung am Abend mitteilte, gab der Student eine verwirrende Darstellung der Vorgänge. Vermutlich sei er geistesgestört, hieß es in einem Bericht der Nachrichtenagentur Associated Press. Mit dem Diebstahl habe er nach seinen Angaben gegen den internationalen Kunstbetrieb und die Lebensbedingungen der Türken in der Bundesrepublik einschließlich West-Berlins protestieren wollen.

Der festgenommene soll wegen des Verschwindens-stiften selbst schwerer Diebstahl vorgeführt werden. In der Vernehmung habe er ausgesagt, dem die Wohnung gehabt oder Rückschläge gesten. Auf die Idee zu seiner Aktion sei er im vergangenen Oktober bei einem ersten Besuch in Berlin gekommen. In dem Zeitplan den er für Polizei bei sich trug, habe er vorgesehen, nach dem Diebstahl mit dem Wagen zum nächstgelegenen U-Bahnhof Hacke-

brücke zu fahren und in die Untergrundbahn zu steigen. Auf dem Bahnhof Kottbusser Tor wollte er den Zug verlassen und die ihm bekannte türkische Familie aufsuchen. In einer Erklärung, die er zuvor verfaßt hatte, heißt es unter anderem:

„Zum Anlaß zu dieser Aktion kam ich seitens meines Aufenthalts in Berlin, im Oktober 1976.

Dies ist der Grund, warum diese Aktion in Berlin stattfindet und konzeptgemäß eine Authenzität festgelegt ist. Die generelle Motivation trifft aber ... den gesamten internationalen Kunstbetrieb zu.

Ich markiere drei maßgebende Kulturinstitute, zwischen diesen bewege ich mich mit einer Reproduktion des Gemäldes von Carl Spitzweg „Der arme Poet". Das Original befindet sich in der Neuen Nationalgalerie, das dritte der markierten Institute.

Das genannte Gemälde ist als Modell im Rahmen der Aktion zu sehen. Gemäß meiner Kritik versetze ich das Gemälde aus dem Kontext der neuen Nationalgalerie (Museum Funktion) in die Situation der Wohnung einer türkischen Gastarbeiterfamilie.

Der Aspekt „Kriminelle Berührung" ist nicht in der Form der Aktion zu sehen, sondern in den Punkten, der mittels der Aktion aufgerufenen Kritik im Bereich der Kulturinstitute, deren Aufgabe und Funktion, als auch im Sinne einer Kunstkritik.

Für die Bichtigkeit und Schwergewicht dieser Kritik findet innerhalb dieser Aktion eine Grenzüberschreitung statt, ich trete als Künstler aus der Projektion des Kunst/Künstlerbereichs in einen offenen Lebensbereich über.

Die Neue Nationalgalerie der Staatlichen Museen Preußischer Kulturbesitz wurde 1965 bis 1968 erbaut. Schwerpunkte der Gemälde, Skulpturen und Handzeichnungen des 19. und 20. Jahrhunderts sind die deutsche Romantik, der Realismus, Impressionismus, Expressionismus und Kunst der Gegenwart.

L. R.

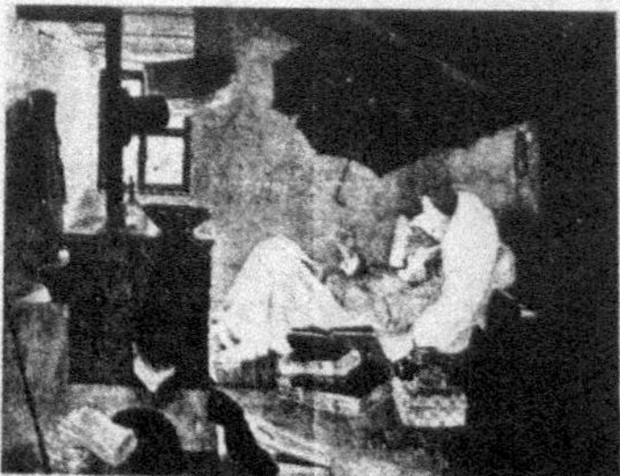
Der Zufall führte Regie: vier Stunden nach der Rückgabe von Carl Spitzwegs „Der arme Poet" war das Gemälde im ZDF-„Hofkonzert" zu sehen.

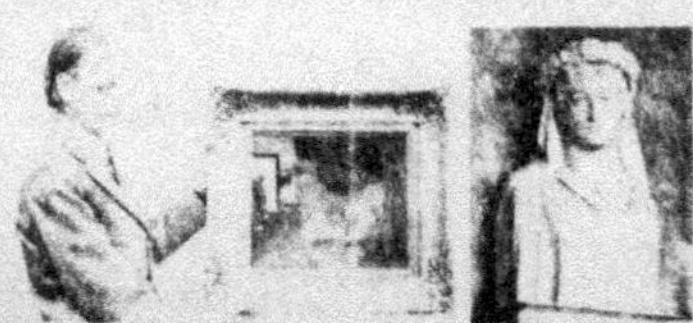
Gestern nachmittag hatte die Museumsleitung den „Armen Poeten" wieder. Rechts: Ähnlich und: 1942 der Diebstahl einer Büste der Königin Luise.

Der kurze Ausflug des „armen Poeten"

Spitzweg-Gemälde für Stunden aus der Nationalgalerie entwendet — Als Kunst- und Sozialkritik hingestellt

Appelle an die Besucher oder: Auf einen Spitzweg spuckt man nicht!

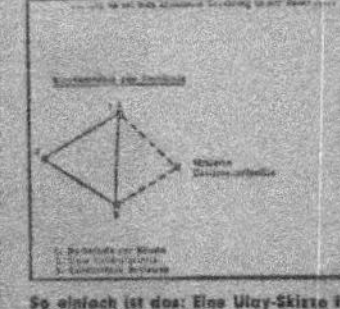

So einfach ist das: Eine Ulay-Skizze für die Spitzweg-Entführung

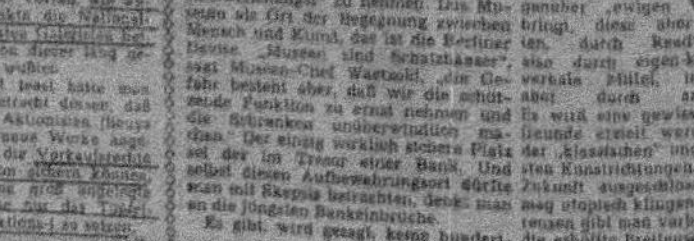

Übers Ziel hinaus

chapter 5

MARINA'S
VIEW OF THE ACTION

I met Ulay in the Appel Gallery when I'd just arrived from Belgrade. There he was. I was preparing myself to do the performance [*Lips of Thomas*, which involved consuming a kilogram of honey and a liter of wine and cutting a star in her stomach, before whipping herself and lying on a cross made of ice with a heater above it] in a gallery for this TV show, the first one that was made about body art. It was called "body art" in those days. Ulay arrived at the gallery and he had this long coat with the fur and half of his face made up like a woman, half as a man. And he was looking fantastic. I mean, come on, coming from fucking communism, I never saw anything like that. I was like, "wow." It was so attractive, really. And then I made the performance. I was cutting my stomach and afterward he really was so gentle, he helped me with the wounds, put alcohol on them and bandages. And then we disappeared.

That same evening, there was a celebration for all the people who worked on this project. We went to a Turkish restaurant to have dinner. And it was my birthday.

And I said to everybody, "Let's have drink, it's my birthday."

And Ulay stood up and said, "It's my birthday too."

And I said, "I don't trust you. You should prove it."

And he came with his diary with November 30 missing. And I could not believe it, I had the same diary, November 30 was missing [in my diary too] because my birthday has always been shitty for me. My mother always told me that I was born on November 29, which is the Day of the Republic [a Yugoslav national holiday], and all the kids born on the 29th go to visit Tito [the beloved former ruler of Yugoslavia], sit on his lap, and get candies and presents. And every time this date came around, my mother said I was not good enough to be invited [that I'd been too naughty]. So I never was invited. Then I finally realized that I was not born on the 29th, I was born 30th, that this is why I was never invited, and she used this as a way of punishment. So I hated my birthdays, and Ulay didn't like his either.

And that night, I mean after the dinner, we just went to his home and we stayed in bed for ten days. It was very passionate, lots of sex, and then I had to go home. I was also married, a little bit married, but I was lovesick [in love with Ulay]. I spent three months away and I was calling him all the time. We recorded all the calls. We have them. We have this recording from Belgrade in audiocassettes. Unbelievable. All this love. Wow wow wow. But then after that, the bill for the telephone was too high. My mother took this old telephone, put it in the cupboard and closed it, so I could not call.

Then we decided we're going to meet in Prague, which is a geographical middle point between Belgrade and Amsterdam. He took a KLM flight and he arrived on time, and I took Aeroflot, the Russian airline, and was six hours late.

He waited for me.

And then we went to the only hotel we could afford, Hotel Paris, which was totally fucked up, and I remember there was the radio that you could never switch off because it was also recording the conversations [of the hotel guests].

Then we decide we would live together. So I went back to Belgrade and I took only my negatives, no clothes, nothing else, got on a second-class train, and I went to Amsterdam. My mother went to the police and said that I was missing. And the police asked, "But how old is your daughter?"

She said, "Twenty-nine."

They said, "Mrs. Abramović, it's about time. We have better stuff to do, please go home."

And that was the end of the story. Then we started living together. And so it was also the start of the story.

MARINA ON THE THEFT

We should start by thinking about why Ulay would want to do that. I think the reason, and this is very interesting, began when we started our relationship. Each of us came with our own language. I came with the language of performance and he came with the language of photography, specifically of Polaroids. He had very few performances in life to that point, maybe one or two, maximum. Everything else was photographic. This was work for which the public was not present in any possible way. He wanted to do something to equalize our relationship and to add performance to his agenda.

When I decided to leave Yugoslavia and to work and live with him, I needed to make three performances. That was a kind of goodbye. One was *Freeing the Voice*, in which I screamed until I couldn't scream anymore. One was *Freeing the Memory*, in which I told the words that I can't remember anymore, for some four hours, everything that came into my head. The last one was also in Berlin. This was *Freeing the Body*, where I have the black scar on my face, I'm naked, I have an African drummer, he was drumming, and I was just moving my body until I couldn't move anymore, and after six hours I collapsed. This was all done before *Irritation* [which Marina refers to as "the Spitzweg"], and in this period he wanted to do something also in Berlin. To do something yes, but he had no idea what at that point. So I can't really tell for sure if he had this idea before our relationship began or not. I would be interested to learn this, because I remember that he started talking about the Spitzweg and talking about Hitler, and that *The Poor Poet* was Hitler's favorite painting, and that Spitzweg painted three versions of the work, not just one, and that there's some replica in Munich and one somewhere else. I didn't know the whole story, but that painting was, for me, just horrible kitsch, really looking horrible. The painter presented this poet in his bed, with a little umbrella because everything's raining and collapsing and poverty and so on.

I remember those days when he got more and more enthusiastic about the idea. We went to the museum many times. It was several months we were in Berlin. He went alone and he went with me too. He really was studying. He had the entire diary written out, including the timing when the guards were changing, how many minutes there was nobody in the basement at which point the Spitzweg was alone, all of this kind of stuff. And about the fire exit. But the main thing for him was to study how many minutes he needed from the basement to get out to the exit. I don't remember anymore but there's something very short, a minute that you have and that's all. That's why the shoes are so important, to run.

He really wanted to plan it like a bank robbery. It was very important for him, the timing; when the guards are going, coming, changing in the museum, how the guards look, are they young, are they old, to understand if they have weapons, if they don't have weapons. Also all the fire exits, the revolving door in the middle of the museum, and when the public is the most there, on the weekends or during the working day. He was also thinking about how he should dress, I don't know, in Adidas sneakers that are fast so he can run. But at the same time, it was the middle of winter, so we also have to think about whether he's going to slip. It was very important to him that, if he takes this painting from the wall, that it will not be damaged, because it's really priceless. So for him, it was very important that the art was not damaged. The concept was important but not to the extent of damaging the art piece.

A part of all this was this problem with the car, because we had a shitty car, it never started when we wanted it to, especially not in the winter. So here his solution was to actually leave the car running, to avoid the problem with it not starting. Because if a guard is running after you and it won't start, he'll just get you. There was so much planning involved. Then we went to René Block, whose gallery in those days represented Sigmar Polke, Nam June Paik, and Joseph Beuys and all these people, to tell him about the idea, which he referred to as the action, *aktion* in German. He was pretty impressed, but also he was not happy to know about it, because it was really breaking the law. So he knew it, but he didn't want to do anything about it or tell anybody. At the same time, he hated that he actually had to keep the secret. I'm not totally sure about this part because Ulay was speaking in German so much in those days. Ulay wanted to make sure that this action was his own work and it was nothing to do with my work. I was finishing my *Body*, *Voice*, and *Memory*, and he was doing his Spitzweg, which was something to do with his childhood. His relatives had been Nazis, he'd been born with the swastika on his birth certificate. So that was really his thing, and I just wanted to be somebody who just recorded the moment.

We had a lawyer already. He actually gave all the information to the lawyer, stating that "this is art action," and so on. So that he would be somehow protected, clear that he didn't actually want to steal the painting to keep it or sell it.

My function at that time . . . I'm so bad at anything technological. I'm bad at opening the telephone, computer, finding anything, and I was very, very worried about my part. But my part was really to have a separate camera and to film that moment when he's taking stuff from the wall. Then immediately take this cassette, put it in my boot, and then put a new one into the camera, so when the police come, I'd say "actually I was filming the police coming." Everybody in the museum saw me with a camera, so the police came straight to me and told me to give them the material. I immediately took the cassette from the camera and gave them this cassette, so they thought they had confiscated evidence. But that new cassette only had a video in which they could see themselves coming to the scene.

It was really a feeling of, "wow, we know we're breaking the law," and it was so much intensity.

Ulay really wanted to document this all well. He found the Fassbinder filmmaker. The cameraman who actually was immediately interested, because for him anything to do with Fassbinder was always edgy, whatever he was doing. He was excited to be involved, so he said yes immediately. I didn't ever have contact with him, I never met him.

That day was especially cold. I remember waking in the morning and being incredibly nervous, both of us hardly talking, dressing, going to the museum. Then when we entered the museum, it started snowing.

Inside, not too many people. I don't think it was more than twelve, maximum eleven, twelve people, and all different types. There was an old couple, there was somebody with a child, there were just random people. The Spitzweg was down in a lower floor, not on the ground floor. Everything had to be very fast. He had to take it, put it in a plastic bag, and run, and he had to break the fire exit, which was next to the revolving door.

I remember I filmed that moment. I put the cassette in and I went immediately upstairs, and the alarm sounded right away. I saw an entire family stuck in the revolving door. With two children. It was a strange image of a frozen family in the entrance and then total chaos, the alarm and running guards.

I saw one guard run very close behind Ulay outside, and I was so afraid that he had a pistol, that he might shoot him. But the good thing about this was that all the guards were old. And that was good, because he easily could run away.

He went into the car, it was running, and the guy that was filming caught this on camera. All of this part I could not see, because basically the car was around the other side of the museum and I was still inside, so I only saw Ulay running, and I saw the guard running. And I saw that Ulay just kind of went faster, so the guard gave up, so the guard was coming back inside, so I knew that Ulay was in the car.

After that, everything froze. The police came very soon, and nobody could leave the museum because we were all stuck. Then they came to me and I gave them the videocassette. After that, we all had to sit down and give statements, which was incredible. It was an event was like a Kurosawa film, *Rashomon*, where you have seven people in the forest, and each of them saw part of a killing and they sit around the fire and tell the story, and every story is completely different, and you can't make any sense of it, even though they were all eyewitnesses. This was exactly like this.

Somebody said he was small with glasses, another one said he was tall and with long hair, another one said, "No, he was bald." It was a description of so many different people but very little to do with the real Ulay. We could not leave for three, four hours. So I had no idea how far he had gone with this action. The idea had been that he would go to the Kreuzberg neighborhood and find a telephone booth and phone the director of the museum and tell him that this is an art action [not a crime]. Then he would go to a Turkish family that he had visited before and take their kitsch from the living room wall, and then put the Nazi kitsch on the wall in its place, and then invite them to sit together.

Ulay really succeeded in getting to Kreuzberg, and he found the telephone box. You can see from the movie. He was so nervous, his voice was different. It was unbelievably romantic because there was snow everywhere, snow that started getting more and more dense. I remember looking later at the movie, when he called the museum and said that the work was not damaged, and they had to come to see it. Of course, in those days the museum director, he was with an assistant, and the police were informed. Later on in the newspaper, in the tabloids, it was said that "leftist radical robbed one of our most beautiful paintings." So this horrible Spitzweg became "one of the most beautiful and treasured paintings."

So the authorities went to this Turkish family, they completely surround the whole Kreuzberg area with the police and such. Ulay never met the director, because he never came. I don't know what happened with the director.

I think the police arrested him. Ulay went to prison. The lawyer was there, so everything was made clear that this was an artistic action. But it was incredibly heroic. I was very proud of him, and that was really the moment that our relationship got in total balance, because of this.

He was forbidden to come to the Neue Nationalgalerie forever, expelled from the museum. But then, a few years later, they put in a glass over the Spitzweg. Somebody actually spit on it, people start spitting on Spitzweg, because they became aware that this was Hitler's favorite painting. And then I think seven years later or something, somebody in a wheelchair stole the Spitzweg, but for real. So the Spitzweg is gone. Who was in the wheelchair? Probably some ex-Nazi who wanted to have it in his bedroom. I have no idea, but this was really an enigma that finally somebody really stole it.

MARINA ON THEIR TIME IN BERLIN

In this period we didn't sell anything. We never thought of the existence of a market or such a thing. It was totally unknown to us. After I made *Rhythm 0* with its seventy-two objects, I asked the director of the gallery to throw everything away, all the objects. I didn't want to have any relics. And if I have to redo the piece, I will literally go and buy the objects anew and put them there. But the director didn't listen to me. So he kept three, four, five things. We are still fighting over them. So when I actually donate this piece to the Museum of Modern Art in Ljubljana, I actually made the shopping list of seventy-two objects, and we just bought the pieces new. And now we have an additional three, and the Tate Modern also bought it.

I don't care. I hated relics.

There was a big exhibition in the Museum of Contemporary Art in Los Angeles, and Paul Schimmel, the chief curator, he came to Ulay and me and asked about the car—the black van—because the car was not only where we lived at the time but also where we worked and we made the performances with this car. He was making a very interesting show, the first of that kind of show, called *Out of Actions*. Let's say Gina Pane, the French artist, if she will cut anything on her body, she will have a piece of white cloth, and make the print, there will be a bloodstain, and that was the project. Chris Burden, in *Trans-Fixed*, worked on a Volkswagen, and the two golden nails that he used to crucify himself, they were in a box. You could buy that for $2,000 at the time. But anyway, so that was all part of the show. Lots of pieces. But we didn't have anything, no relics. The only thing was the car.

Eventually, when we stopped living in the car and we went to Australia, we sold it. We sold the car to an Amsterdam filmmaker, who was using it to transport rails from city to city. We told Paul Schimmel what we knew. He started searching for the car. He found the guy in Amsterdam, but this guy said, "I sold to somebody in the south of France," so he was like a shriveled corpse. He went to the south of France and found the car that wasn't working anymore, but it was in a backyard. They kept chickens inside it. He was so crazy that he bought the car back for the museum, cleaned the chicken shit—which was not easy—and brought the car to Los Angeles. So we had the car in that show, which is a really important show. Then that car went to Japan, to the National Museum of Modern Art. From Japan, it went to Lyon, and Lyon bought the car. So now for this new show, which I call "ART VITAL," the car is coming. It's going to absolutely be in the exhibition. Also, I showed the same car at MoMA. To me, when I arrived and Ulay was there at MoMA, and we saw this car . . . that car was it, we were living literally homeless in it, and now it's in the Museum of Modern Art. It was a long road it traveled.

But at that time, with the Spitzweg action, the only thing that we were interested in was documentation. Documentation was everything, but not because we were going to sell it. It was just that it was the only proof that the action was made. So Ulay kept all the newspapers that wrote on it, like tabloids with these crazy titles. He kept the documentation. He also kept the conversation from the phone call. I think he taped himself. And that was it. So what is left to sell? The film. But in that time, really selling work was absolutely not even something we thought about. The only time that we started selling work was when we started making these large Polaroids. That was the first time that we sold anything. And we started selling at the end of our relationship too. Because somehow without money, it was more united.

MARINA ON RELICS OF PERFORMANCE

One of the most famous performances I made is *The Artist Is Present*. When I finished the performance, I made one photographic work, nothing to do with this performance, just me carrying wood. Lots of wood, because artists have to also know how to make fire. It was a very big print, and I made thirty-five of them and I sold them for $15,000 each, which is the cheapest for that size of the print. The galleries were selling for me without taking any percentage. It's just print money to have to use so that I can have somebody for one year actually putting all this material together [the masses of video material from *The Artist Is Present*], because I have a real live recording. Every single person [was filmed sitting opposite me] in real time. I mean, we're talking 1,560 people. On one side was only the people looking at me in real time, on the other side was all me looking at them, also in real time. This was a huge installation that I just showed now at MoMA. And then I kept the table and the two chairs. The museum never bought them. I still have them. And everybody said that it was such an important action, but it's very difficult to sell. I made this because I want to have the real-time recording. You don't need to see it, but you know that it's real. Especially for a long durational work, I'm always making them in real time. But to sell, like I'm selling photographic work, I'm selling now objects that are actually transitory, the public can use them, all made with minerals.

But from all of these performances, I sold Tate Modern *Rhythm 0*, but this is after thirty years, because now the people are into vintage. Now the people are interested in very vintage photographs, why they are so messed up, so full of yellow, because time passed by. They don't care. Now they want to have this material. But when we were making things at the time, we artists had no knowledge at all.

I come from communism and every recording can be evidence. So I record everything. My mother [Danica Rosić] was the director of the Museum of Revolution [in Belgrade]. Everything was recorded. So I had this in my cells, my DNA. And Ulay was a photographer, deeply, in his blood, so he was always photographing, he was photographing landscapes, people, stuff, whatever. So somehow both of us have this. I was early, so all my performances are perfectly recorded. If I didn't have any money for Super 8 at that time, there was photographic work, but as much time I spent having an idea, I spent thinking, "how is this idea going to be recorded?" Like *Rhythm 10*. For *Rhythm 10* [a performance that involves rapidly stabbing a knife between her splayed fingers], I don't have any video, but I have sound; audiocassettes were cheaper. So I have the sound of knives going between my fingers, I recorded the whole situation. So it's a very clear sequence, you can see it [by hearing it]. In the past, photographers always asked to come record performances, but nobody was giving any instructions to the photographers, and that was the real problem. So let's say Joseph Beuys's [1965] piece called *How to Explain Pictures to a Dead Hare*, for this there were four or five photographers, and they would come photograph left to the right, then they smoke cigarettes, come back in, and take some more, and they would have these old photographs. And then Beuys would look at them and say, of all these "only one image is going to present the work."

And now Beuys's widow, she had the royalty court cases because all of these photographers consider this as their own work, that it's their own vision of the thing. It's complicated, but my knowledge of especially videos came from very interesting story, when I was invited in Denmark in 1975 to make the piece called *Art Must Be Beautiful, Artist Must Be Beautiful*. Combing my hair, damaging my face. This was the first time I was proposed to make video. Video didn't exist in ex-Yugoslavia. So I didn't have any idea what I'm supposed to tell to the guy about how to record it. I was so excited. I made the performance for the public, he recorded it. The public left immediately, and I went to see the material. When I saw the material, I was absolutely disgusted. The guy was using every possibility, every filmmaker's tool: solarization, moving camera, focus in, focus out, filming my feet when I was doing my hair. I told him, "can you show me where's the delete button?" And he said, "this one" and I pressed delete and I deleted the entire piece. And I say to him, "this was my learning process." Then I said to him, "Okay, so I'm going to repeat this entire performance now for the camera. The camera is my public. I'm going to create the frame and then all that you have to do is press the record button and go and smoke cigarettes." And he did, and from that time on, my own recordings are perfect because I knew how to do it.

But the problem generally with this work, and with so many artists who had wonderful works, is that they're recorded with just shitty black-and-white video. Starting from the conscious, starting from all of these people, they represent amazing material, but bad-quality video because a good one was not available or cost too much. And now you have all this cheap equipment, all the Instagram great images with no content, totally horrible ideas, so you have this glittery stuff of bad work and great stuff with shitty recordings.

chapter 6

ART THEFT AS CRIME

One year after the "Berlin lifting," so it's 1977.

Ulay and Abramović are cold, broke, and exhausted. They're holed up in Wiesbaden, visiting a wealthy collector friend named Michael Berger. It's bleak. The streets are iced over, the skies gray and unrelenting. "Wiesbaden was so miserable," Ulay remembers. "Everything frozen, the roads, the air—we were miserable, poor, still living in our van."[1]

They need escape. Something warm. Something far.

"We need some sun," they say.

Berger, generous and flush with money, offers a gift: two plane tickets, anywhere they want. No catch. Just choose a destination and go.

They choose Morocco.

Berger books the tickets. The flight leaves from Frankfurt, but with one inconvenient detail: a stopover in Munich. Just a routine transfer. Or so they think.

But in Munich, fate catches up.

The stop, for some unfathomable reason, routes them through customs. A border officer thumbs through a thick black book—nothing digital, just a list of names. And there it is.

"And they caught me," Ulay sighs.

He's standing still, then suddenly surrounded. There's no escape this time. "I thought I got away with it," he says. He hadn't. They arrest him on the spot. The charge was failure to serve his sentence. The punishment was thirty-six days' imprisonment or 3,600 Deutschmarks.

It hits like a slap. Inevitable, but still a surprise.

Ulay dials Berger from Munich. "Michael, I got a big problem, you know. . . . I got arrested again."

Berger doesn't hesitate. He dispatches his brother, who lives nearby, to bail Ulay out. Just like that, Ulay walks free.

For now.

He skips bail. Morocco disappears into a puff of missed chance. The debt—legal, financial, karmic—still lingers, unpaid.

—

Back in Amsterdam, the story takes another twist.

Ulay is summoned to the German consulate. A plain room. A stern diplomat. Ulay pleads his case—he's an artist, broke, idealistic, living on fumes and ideas. He can't pay 3,600 Deutschmarks.

The consul isn't moved.

"That's no good," he says flatly. "Sooner or later . . . they will get you."

He's right.

Some months later, Ulay boards a train heading toward the German border. As the train slows at the checkpoint, he feels it before it happens. Officers move through the cars. They reach him. Pull him off.

Arrested. Again.

This time, they don't treat him as a performance artist—or even a petty thief. They classify him as a "social delinquent" and send him to what he calls a *terrorist prison*.

"It was unbelievable," Ulay says. Concrete walls. Steel doors. Time to think.

He serves ten or maybe fourteen days. He loses count. But he makes the most of it.

—

So in the end, yes—the action was punished. Not severely. Not forever. But enough to leave a bruise. A brush with something harder than politics or aesthetics.

And yet what lives on isn't the sentence, it's the story. The action. The myth.

The "Berlin lifting" as it is sometimes called becomes one of the most legendary acts in the history of performance art—though Ulay himself resisted calling it a performance. He preferred *aktion*. Something demonstrative. Something real.

Still, the art world remembers it as a kind of masterpiece of conceptual theater: part heist, part protest, part parable. We'll examine those concepts next.

And then comes the ironic punchline. The kind that a screenwriter wouldn't dare invent.

This time, it's not an artist making a statement. It's just two guys—one in a wheelchair, the other pushing it. They enter Schloss Charlottenburg and go straight to the painting. The same painting that once hung in Berlin, that was once "lifted" by Ulay. No subtlety. They yank it from the wall, bludgeon a guard with the heavy frame, knock him unconscious, and vanish into the Berlin streets.

No manifesto. No cameras. No call to the police.

Just gone.

The painting has never been recovered.

Only this time, Ulay didn't do it.

—

That second theft? It's worth exploring more deeply.

In the hushed galleries of Berlin's Schloss Charlottenburg, a brazen theft unfolded on September 3, 1989. Two men, one feigning disability in a red wheelchair, maneuvered through the Galerie der Romantik. Their target was Carl Spitzweg's cherished painting *The Poor Poet*. As they approached the artwork, they swiftly removed it from the wall. When a security guard confronted them, they assaulted him and fled, leaving behind the wheelchair—a mere prop in their audacious plan. Despite the alarm sounding and the guard's injuries, the thieves vanished without a trace, taking with them not only *The Poor Poet* but also another Spitzweg masterpiece, *The Love Letter*. To this day, both paintings remain missing.[2]

The version of Carl Spitzweg's *The Poor Poet* stolen in 1989 from Berlin's Schloss Charlottenburg is the same painting that was temporarily taken by Ulay in 1976. This particular version, one of three created by Spitzweg in 1839, was housed in the Neue Nationalgalerie in Berlin at the time of Ulay's performance. After the 1976 event, the painting was returned unharmed and later transferred to Schloss Charlottenburg, where it remained until its theft in 1989.[3]

The 1989 theft, however, was a calculated crime with no artistic intent. The perpetrators exploited the museum's security vulnerabilities, using deception and violence to achieve their goal. The fact that they left behind the wheelchair suggests a level of premeditation and confidence in their plan. Despite investigations, no substantial leads have emerged, and the paintings have not resurfaced on the art market.

The permanent (at least to date) loss of *The Poor Poet* is not just the disappearance of a physical artwork but a cultural tragedy. The painting encapsulates a significant part of German artistic heritage, reflecting societal values and historical contexts. Its absence leaves a void in the narrative of German art history. It is also deeply ironic that it should be the same work stolen as artistic action later stolen as simple crime.

Efforts to recover the stolen paintings continue. However, the passage of time diminishes the likelihood of recovery. The art world remains hopeful, as history has shown that stolen artworks can resurface decades later.

The 1989 theft of *The Poor Poet* stands as a stark reminder of the vulnerabilities of cultural institutions and the enduring impact of art on national identity. The painting's dual history—first as a subject of performance art and later as a victim of criminal theft—underscores its significance and the profound loss its absence represents.

—

It may seem so obvious that art theft is a crime that it doesn't warrant mentioning. But in the context of this book, about an art theft as artwork, it is worth spending a chapter grounding ourselves in art theft through history, which is effectively the context in which Ulay's action took place.

The art heist is an act of theater. It is performance, choreography, and spectacle. But while a handful of art crimes have been undertaken with artistic intent (of which more in the next chapter), the vast majority of art thefts are not performances but crimes. And yet they borrow the language of performance: They involve disguises and rehearsals, often follow scripts borrowed from cinema, and are consumed by the public as thrilling spectacles. This chapter explores that theater of art theft, not as artistic expression but as crime—precise, calculated, and theatrical nonetheless.

We begin, appropriately, with smoke and mirrors.

On August 6, 2010, fog hung thick over Stockholm. That stillness was shattered by car bombs exploding across the city. Sirens wailed, emergency responders scrambled, and chaos reigned. But the bombs were a decoy. The real target was the Chinese Pavilion on the grounds of Drottningholm Palace. A band of thieves used the commotion as cover to break into the royal residence and steal seven Chinese antiquities, including a lacquered chalice, a rhinoceros horn goblet, and a musk wood plate. It took them six minutes. They escaped first by moped, then by boat across Lake Mälaren, vanishing into the mist.[4]

These thieves knew exactly what they wanted: Chinese imperial treasures, many of which had once been looted by Europeans from Beijing's Old Summer Palace during the Second Opium War in 1860. The objects taken from Drottningholm were of the same ilk. This was not a theft of convenience. It was precise, symbolic, and efficient.

The Stockholm heist kicked off a series of thefts targeting Chinese antiquities from European museums. In Durham, Norwich, Cambridge, Fontainebleau, Valladolid, and Bergen, objects with similar provenance disappeared. In Bergen, the KODE Art Museum—a white block of a building styled with ersatz Chinese temple features—was hit twice, in 2010 and again in 2013. The second theft was amateurish: The culprits smashed display cases, left DNA evidence, and damaged many of the fragile artifacts they tried to steal. But still, none of the stolen objects were recovered.[5]

Kenneth Didriksen of the Norwegian police suspected these were "thefts to order," fulfilling a demand within the Chinese art market for repatriated imperial objects. Yet the clumsiness of the 2013 Bergen crew suggests they were opportunists rather than professionals, perhaps responding to criminal rumors that someone was buying Chinese antiquities rather than acting under direct commission. In this, they echo the aspirations of many art thieves: acting under the illusion that some wealthy, hidden collector waits in the wings.

This illusion—of the mysterious buyer, the refined criminal, the Thomas Crown or Dr. No of art crime lore—has long shaped both the public perception and the criminal practice of art theft. But such figures are more fiction than fact. There are only a few dozen known instances in which criminal collectors commissioned art thefts, despite tens of thousands of thefts reported annually. Yet criminals continue to believe in them—and police, aware of this, often use sting operations with undercover officers posing as such buyers to recover stolen works.

That very tactic helped solve another cinematic heist: the 2000 robbery of Stockholm's Nationalmuseum. On that day, three men in balaclavas stormed the museum with submachine guns. As they grabbed a Rembrandt and other paintings, their accomplices set off car bombs across the city to distract the police. Tire spikes scattered in the streets delayed pursuit. The thieves escaped by speedboat. It was a movie heist in real life—until they tried to sell the art. The Rembrandt was ultimately recovered when a thief offered it to an undercover policeman posing as a shady art collector.[6]

Sometimes the heists are grand but the thieves are mundane. In 1986, Martin "The General" Cahill, a notorious Irish gangster, raided Russborough House near Dublin, stealing eighteen paintings, including Vermeer's *Lady Writing a Letter with Her Maid*. But Cahill found no buyer. Instead he used the Vermeer as collateral for a $1 million loan from a crooked Antwerp diamond dealer. The money bought heroin, which the gang sold on the street. The plan was to repay the loan and reclaim the Vermeer—but the diamond dealer had other ideas. He tried to sell it and instead sold it to Charlie Hill, an undercover Scotland Yard officer.[7]

These are a select few among the innumerable art theft cases one could call upon. They have been chosen here to highlight a persistent pattern. Art thieves often do not understand how difficult it is to sell stolen art. They rely on fantasies drawn from books and films. They imagine ransoms will be paid or that black market collectors exist in numbers. When those hopes fail, the works sit unsold or are used as criminal currency—traded for drugs or weapons or as loan collateral.

The theft of Gainsborough's *Portrait of Georgiana, Duchess of Devonshire* in 1876 established many of these tropes. Adam Worth, the model for Sir Arthur Conan Doyle's Professor Moriarty, stole it not to sell but to blackmail a gallerist. The plan failed, so Worth kept the painting for decades, eventually selling it to J. P. Morgan to fund his retirement. Worth forbade his men from carrying weapons. He was clever, disciplined, and saw himself as a gentleman thief.[8]

Then came the *Mona Lisa*.

In 1911, Vincenzo Peruggia, a handyman working at the Louvre, hid in a closet overnight, removed Leonardo's *Mona Lisa* from the wall and its frame, wrapped it in a white sheet, and tried to leave through a side door. But it was locked. He removed the doorknob, failed to open it, and had to wait for a janitor to let him out. Two years later, he brought the painting to Florence, believing he would be hailed a national hero for "returning" it to Italy. Instead he was arrested. Peruggia genuinely thought Napoleon had looted the painting, though in truth it had been acquired legally centuries earlier.

In these stories, the motivations range from ideological to financial to deeply personal. But what links them is the performative nature of the thefts themselves: elaborate preparations, a sense of mission, and an often mistaken belief in a receptive, even admiring audience. As we shall see in later sections, this belief sometimes edges into self-delusion—or, in the case of artists like Ulay, into intentional, artistic transgression.

For now, we remain in the realm of theft as theft. But already the lines blur. When Peruggia smuggled the *Mona Lisa* back to Italy, he saw himself not as a thief but as a patriot. When Worth refused violence and treated art with reverence, he played the part of a gentleman. And when thieves set off car bombs to steal Chinese antiquities, they reenacted a historical drama of looting and loss, inverting past crimes under the cover of fog.

HITLER'S AESTHETIC OBSESSION

In his youth, Adolf Hitler dreamed not of conquest but of canvas. At eighteen, he arrived in Vienna with a portfolio of architectural renderings and romantic landscapes, hoping to gain admission to the prestigious Academy of Fine Arts. He failed. Twice. His application was rejected in 1907 and again in 1908—not because he lacked diligence but because he lacked talent. A professor reportedly remarked that Hitler had skill in architectural draftsmanship but no understanding of the human form. The academy suggested he try the School of Architecture, but he lacked the secondary education to qualify.[9]

Thus began a lifelong tension between artistic aspiration and aesthetic control. Rebuffed by the art world he so revered, Hitler became its most infamous looter. His failures as an artist were not merely formative, they were foundational. They gave rise to a worldview in which art was not only a reflection of racial ideology but also an object of conquest.

This personal fixation took institutional form in the planned Führermuseum in Linz, Austria—Hitler's adopted hometown. The museum was to be a shrine to German culture and a testament to Hitler's curatorial authority. Designed to eclipse the Louvre, the Prado, and the Hermitage, it would house the greatest collection of art in the world—acquired not through patronage or purchase but by theft.

The scale of the project was staggering. Architectural plans envisioned a grand neoclassical complex dominating the Danube, its galleries filled with works by artists Hitler admired—German masters like Albrecht Dürer and Hans Holbein, but also select Italians (Michelangelo, Leonardo), Dutch painters (Rembrandt, Vermeer), and even French neoclassicists like David and Ingres. What it would not contain were modernists, abstractionists, or Jewish artists. Hitler, like Stalin, saw modern art as degenerate, the aesthetic equivalent of moral decay. His preferences froze somewhere around 1850, with a nostalgic tilt toward the serene, the orderly, and the idealized.[10]

To populate this future museum, the Nazi state launched the most ambitious art looting campaign in history. At its center was the Einsatzstab Reichsleiter Rosenberg, or ERR, a Nazi task force named after ideologue Alfred Rosenberg and charged with the cultural plunder of occupied Europe. Formed in 1940, the ERR operated with bureaucratic efficiency and ideological zeal, targeting private Jewish collections, Freemason libraries, and institutions deemed politically or racially suspect.

The ERR's headquarters were in Paris, at the Jeu de Paume museum, where looted art was processed like seized contraband. There, Nazi curators such as Bruno Lohse cataloged masterpieces by Renoir, Cézanne, Matisse, and Picasso—many from the collections of Jewish families like the Rothschilds, the Wildensteins, and the Rosenbergs. Paintings deemed "degenerate" were earmarked for destruction or sale to fund the Reich, while works considered museum-worthy were crated and shipped to Germany, often with Linz as their final destination.[11]

A surreal image emerges from the archives: rows of paintings leaning against the walls of the Jeu de Paume, swastikas fluttering overhead, while officers in SS uniforms debated the relative merits of Rubens versus Goya. Hitler himself reviewed photo albums of confiscated works, placing checkmarks next to the ones he wanted for his museum. His agents followed suit, scouring mansions, bank vaults, and abandoned châteaux across the continent. Entire trainloads of art were diverted from Allied bombing raids and rerouted into tunnels in the Austrian Alps, stored in salt mines under mountains near Altaussee.

This convergence of personal taste and imperial policy was not unique to Hitler—it has echoes in the collections of monarchs, popes, and robber barons—but never before had aesthetic preference become a justification for armed invasion. Hitler invaded Poland, France, and the Netherlands with tanks and artillery, but also with packing crates and condition reports. His generals looted not just for profit but for praise.

And yet, for all this effort, the Führermuseum was never built. The war turned. The Allies advanced. The troves at Altaussee were discovered by the Monuments Men, a team of art historians and soldiers tasked with recovering stolen cultural property. Among the thousands of works found were Jan van Eyck's *Ghent Altarpiece*, Vermeer's *The Astronomer*, and Michelangelo's *Bruges Madonna*. It was as if the contents of an impossible museum had been hidden in the belly of a mountain, awaiting a curator who would never come.[12]

Hitler's aesthetic vision was not incidental, it was central to his self-image. He saw himself not only as a leader of men but as a guardian of culture, a failed artist elevated to the status of supreme arbiter. Art, for him, was both refuge and weapon: It validated his tastes, reflected his ideology, and helped construct the myth of his destiny. When he couldn't make art, he stole it. Then he buried it in salt and stone, waiting for a future that never arrived.

Hitler's interest in art, and his questionable taste, are what prompted Ulay's choice of target. He would have still stolen art as a performative act regardless, but when selecting the object of his action, the Hitler connection was too juicy to pass over.

—

In 2009, Christie's held a high-profile auction of the estate of Yves Saint Laurent and Pierre Bergé at the Grand Palais in Paris. Among the most anticipated lots were two bronze animal heads: a rat and a rabbit. They had once formed part of a water clock at Beijing's Old Summer Palace, looted by Anglo-French forces in 1860. The bronzes fetched £15 million each, but the sale caused an international uproar. The buyer, Cai Mingchao, was a Chinese art dealer and cultural advisor who had no intention of paying. His bid was a political protest. He believed China should not be forced to buy back its cultural heritage from the West.[13]

This episode was more than just a dramatic gesture. It revealed the intense nationalist sentiment surrounding looted Chinese art—and it coincided almost exactly with the beginning of the wave of Chinese antiquities heists in Europe. Whether or not Cai's actions inspired the thefts, they were part of the same cultural conversation: one about restitution, colonialism, and the value of art as identity. And they bring together the opening part of this chapter, introducing art theft as a criminal enterprise, and the second part, on Hitler's aesthetics and his wish to gather a museum that featured everything that he admired.

But the thefts of Chinese imperial art themselves began to seem like a form of reverse looting—not sanctioned by the state but perhaps encouraged by a shifting cultural climate. Chinese collectors and institutions increasingly sought to reacquire looted treasures, and the booming Chinese art market made such objects immensely valuable. Some believed the Chinese government quietly supported efforts to retrieve lost national heritage, though no official links have been proven.

One of the most dramatic thefts in this category took place at the Musée Chinois in Fontainebleau in 2015. The museum's Chinese Room, filled with imperial objects given to Napoleon III by the Chinese court, was ransacked in minutes. Thieves took twenty-two items, bypassing others of equal or greater value—suggesting they had a shopping list.[14] As in the Drottningholm case, these thieves knew exactly what they wanted. The implication was clear: Someone had told them.

The mystery deepens when we look at a foiled attempt at Fontainebleau in 2019. The same room was targeted again, this time unsuccessfully. Were the same people behind both attempts? Were they returning for what they missed? Or had news of the successful 2015 theft inspired copycats?

A similar ambiguity haunts the cases of thefts in Durham, Norwich, and Cambridge, all involving Chinese antiquities taken from university or regional museums in England. These institutions were targeted for their imperial loot, often held in minimal-security environments. The question, as always, was whether the thefts were connected—and whether the Rathkeale Rovers, a gang of Irish travelers notorious for stealing rhino horn, might also have been involved.

The Rovers, also known as the Dead Zoo Gang, made a fortune breaking into natural history museums and stealing rhinoceros horns. Rhino horn is highly prized in Chinese medicine, and the gang had developed links to Asian buyers. Could they have turned their attention to imperial Chinese art?

The evidence is suggestive, if not conclusive. Many of the heists used similar methods: smash-and-grab attacks, executed in under ten minutes, with little regard for elegance. Yet the objects taken suggest careful planning. These were not random thefts. They followed the rhythms of a market demand.

And the market, like the media, feeds on mythology. The more dramatic the heist, the more valuable the object. Provenance becomes part of the story. A once-forgotten jade sculpture gains new cachet as "the piece stolen in the 2010 Bergen heist."

The media, too, has played a pivotal role. Tabloids celebrate art thieves as folk heroes. Even bumbling criminals like Robert Mang, who drunkenly stole Benvenuto Cellini's gold salt cellar from a Vienna museum, become tabloid darlings. The media portrays them as everymen, poking fun at elite institutions. The subtext is that maybe the museums had it coming.[15]

This narrative extends even to high-stakes international crime. When the Ukrainian painting *The Taking of Christ* by Caravaggio was stolen in 2008, headlines screamed about a $100 million loss. But the painting was a copy, not an original. The real Caravaggio hangs in Dublin. Nonetheless, the thieves—and the media—believed the myth. The inflated value served the criminals well as they sought to use the painting as collateral in the illicit trade.[16]

The media, in effect, helps thieves launder cultural capital. A stolen artwork is not just a commodity, it's a legend in the making. It becomes currency in a story, and in the underworld, story has value.

This final section investigates the liminal zone where theft verges on performance—where the act of stealing becomes itself a statement and the line between criminal and artist begins to blur.

Nowhere is this tension more pronounced than in the case of Stéphane Breitwieser, a French waiter whose compulsive thefts defied logic and economic reasoning. Over a span of seven years, Breitwieser stole an estimated three hundred artworks from museums and galleries across Europe.[17] Yet he never sold a single one. Instead he hoarded them in a secret attic room at his mother's home in Mulhouse. His motive, he claimed, was love—love of art, beauty, and possession. Breitwieser did not consider himself a thief but a collector misunderstood by a society that had commodified what he cherished.

There is something eerily sincere in Breitwieser's obsession. He developed a method, a rhythm: visiting small museums during quiet hours, disabling alarms, slipping artworks under his coat, and walking out. He struck during lunch breaks or rainy weekdays when galleries were underpatrolled. His thefts were surgical, but his motive was deeply personal. When finally caught, the tragedy deepened—his mother, in a panic, destroyed much of his collection, tossing centuries-old paintings into a canal and shoving others into a garbage disposal. It was a moment of iconoclastic violence, driven by panic but resonant with metaphor: beauty lost to fear, artistry obliterated to conceal crime.

Breitwieser's case illustrates a rare but haunting pattern: art stolen not for ransom, not for resale, but for reverie. These thieves are curators of private museums, vaults of desire accessible only to themselves. They are performance artists unaware of their own dramaturgy, their acts choreographed not for the public but for the mirror.

Contrast this with the calculated absurdity of Joseph Honoré Gery Pieret, an associate of Pablo Picasso. Pieret famously stole a series of small Iberian sculptures from the Louvre in the early 1900s—not to profit but to boast. He would sneak them out in his coat, then show them off to friends. Picasso, who purchased at least two of the stolen pieces, later claimed to have been ignorant of their provenance, though the thefts inspired serious self-reflection—and possibly *Les Demoiselles d'Avignon* itself. Pieret's thefts were acts of provocation, not profit. He was a minor thief but a major character, the sort of man who understood art theft as a performance of irreverence.[18]

In other cases, the theatricality lies not in the motive but in the method. In 2002, a group of thieves entered the Van Gogh Museum in Amsterdam by using a ladder. They stole two paintings worth tens of millions of euros—*View of the Sea at Scheveningen* and *Congregation Leaving the Reformed Church in Nuenen*—in under four minutes.[19] The heist was so swift, so stylized, that for years many assumed the works had been stolen to order. The paintings were recovered over a decade later in Naples, stashed in the villa of a mafia boss. It was art as collateral but also as trophy—a performative flex within the shadow economies of crime.

Sometimes it is not just criminals but the institutions themselves that enter the stage. When that Ukrainian Caravaggio copy was stolen in 2008, its value was inflated by media speculation and state silence. Even after its recovery, confusion lingered over its authenticity. Authorities denied and confirmed in equal measure, perhaps understanding that ambiguity could serve national pride better than facts. A lost Caravaggio, after all, attracts more attention than a recovered copy. In this way, art theft becomes not just performance by criminals but a theater of official narratives, competing for authority.

And then there is the art theft that was, in itself, art.

Ulay's theft was not about ownership but authorship. He appropriated an act of crime and reframed it as a critique—of museums, nationalism, and exclusion. The Spitzweg painting, a sentimental icon of nineteenth-century German culture, was relocated from the white cube of institutional prestige to the lived space of a marginalized migrant. The gesture was political, poetic, and pointed. Ulay turned theft into a medium.

In the shadow of this act, all other heists begin to shimmer with ambiguity. Was Peruggia's theft of the *Mona Lisa* a nationalist stunt? Was Cai Mingchao's unpaid bid for the zodiac heads a kind of auction house performance? Can Breitwieser's attic be read as installation art, his hoarding as a form of obsessive curatorship?

What unites these stories is the central paradox of art theft: It is at once a violation and an homage. To steal a painting is to declare it valuable, to remove it from circulation and enshrine it in secrecy. Whether motivated by greed, ideology, or compulsion, the thief becomes a curator of absence. The museum label that reads "stolen" may attract more visitors than the work ever did in situ.

In this way, art theft is a strange form of authorship. The thief remakes the meaning of the object. And in rare instances—like Ulay's—the theft is the artwork.

And the artwork can be stolen from the "thief." Without bringing in too many details, let it be recalled, as Ulay stated to me, that Wilma Kottusch withheld the original copy of the film of the "Berlin lifting." She intervened on several occasions to attempt to block the exhibition of the film—Ulay's copy of the original, which he edited and worked on because she never gave him the original—at some of Ulay's last major retrospectives. More than once the museums stepped in to save the situation, but from an external perspective her actions smack of extortion over an artwork by a great artist in which she was peripherally involved. This stung and haunted Ulay into his final years. The soap opera soured even more when a man who appeared ready to help solve the issue, allying himself to Ulay and appearing to be the white knight, turned out to be playing a game himself. He had acquired the original film from Kottusch and was trying to extort money for himself.

There were contentious periods with Marina, too, and they were much publicized (I broke the news in *The Guardian* about their lawsuit and its outcome). But Marina takes this all in stride. As I write she is working on a catalog of their joint works for the Cukrarna art gallery in Ljubljana and suggested it be called *Love Hate Forgiveness*, which beautifully summarizes their life together. Those writing the catalog were shy about including too much of the "hate" part, but she insisted that it be there, as it was part of their story.

Ownership issues were always going to be tricky among self-proclaimed "hippies," as Ulay described himself and Marina in the 1970s, who didn't think that the work they were creating was going to be of enduring interest, much less a valuable collectible. They just wanted to do things, actions as art. The commodification of it, the very fact that relics (like photographs or video) survive, is almost by accident. Today everything is thoroughly documented, whether it has merit or not, but that was a different time and the protagonists had a different mindset. Thankfully, Ulay's widow, Lena Pislak, champions Ulay's legacy and is dear friends with Marina. Ulay's art is in good hands, protected from further theft attempts.

In the next chapter, we will turn fully to art theft as artistic performance beyond Ulay. But we will carry forward the knowledge gathered here: Even when art is stolen as crime, it is often received—and retold—as spectacle. And every spectacle demands an audience.

chapter 7

ART CRIME AS ART

Art has been stolen for as long as it has held value—whether symbolic, spiritual, or financial. Each year, tens of thousands of art thefts are reported around the world, with countless more slipping under the radar.[1] But the idea of art theft *as* art? That is something new. Or nearly new.

WHEN ARTISTS COMMIT ART CRIME

Art crime is typically imagined as the domain of outsiders: thieves who target museums for loot, forgers who deceive experts, or vandals who scrawl their names on temple walls or smash statue heads. But some of the most subversive, ambiguous, and culturally resonant art crimes have been committed not by criminals but by artists. These acts are not simply transgressions, they are provocations. Their criminality is the medium. Their audience is the institution.

In 1974, the Iranian American artist Tony Shafrazi entered the Museum of Modern Art in New York and approached one of its most prized paintings: Pablo Picasso's *Guernica*. He pulled a can of red spray paint from his jacket and scrawled three words across the canvas: "KILL LIES ALL."[2] It was an act of political protest. Just days earlier, President Richard Nixon had pardoned William Calley, the US Army officer convicted for his role in the My Lai massacre during the Vietnam War. Shafrazi's action was both a critique of American militarism and an ironic echo of the very violence Picasso had condemned in *Guernica*. The painting, meant as a memorial to civilian suffering during the Spanish Civil War, now bore the scars of protest against a contemporary atrocity.

Museum staff and the world of cultured folk were horrified. But the paint had been applied in such a way that it could be cleaned without lasting damage, and Shafrazi was not a madman off the street—he was a young artist working within the tradition of political intervention. "I wanted to bring the art absolutely into the real world," he later said. "To shake people up."[3] Decades later, Shafrazi became a prominent art dealer, representing artists like Keith Haring and Jean-Michel Basquiat. The episode at MoMA remains one of the most iconic acts of performative vandalism in modern art history. It was a crime, certainly. A law was broken and a cultural treasure was defaced, potentially damaging it irrevocably. But it was not designed for personal gain but to make a sociopolitical statement.

In a more intimate but no less radical gesture, Robert Rauschenberg's *Erased de Kooning Drawing* (1953) turned destruction into creation. Rauschenberg, then an ambitious young artist, approached Willem de Kooning—already a towering figure in the Abstract Expressionist movement—and asked him for a drawing.[4] Not to keep. To erase. De Kooning, intrigued, agreed, but he handed over a drawing he said he'd miss, one made in mixed media and therefore difficult to erase. Over the next month, Rauschenberg painstakingly rubbed out every visible mark.

What remained was a nearly blank sheet of paper, framed and titled not by what it showed but by what it no longer did. The drawing was gone, but the act was now art. Rauschenberg had enacted the conceptual death of one generation's hero in order to clear space for his own. It was at once homage, critique, and theft—not of an object but of authorship. He did not vandalize the drawing in a moment of protest; he transformed it through erasure into something new, a palimpsest of power and permission.

Another artist took a more literal approach to violating institutional authority. In the 1990s, the Czech artist Milan Knížák urinated on a painting in a state-run gallery, declaring that "a true artist must challenge what the state presents as culture."[5] In similar spirit, the Russian performance artist Alexander Brener famously defaced Kazimir Malevich's *White Cross on White Background* by spray-painting a green dollar sign over it in 1997.[6] Brener claimed the act was a protest against the commodification of art and the corruption of the art world. He was arrested, sentenced to five months in prison, and banned from Russian museums.

Brener's act exemplifies a subset of art crime: One committed in order to indict the system that defines what is and isn't art. These provocations are less about damage than they are about dissent. They use destruction as a medium, illegality as brushstroke.

A distinction must be made between acts intended to be artistic and acts against art intended simply to get attention because the perpetrators know that attacking art results in media coverage. In recent years, a troubling trend has emerged in which climate activists, in an effort to raise awareness of environmental catastrophe, have thrown soup, mashed potatoes, or glue at famous paintings in prominent museums.[7] While the artworks themselves are usually protected behind glass and remain unharmed, the gesture carries a jarring message: that the value of human cultural heritage can be collateral damage in the fight for a higher moral cause. These acts are designed to provoke outrage and generate headlines, which they certainly do. But they do so at a cost—one not paid by governments or fossil fuel corporations but by the public trust in art institutions and, ultimately, by art itself.

Attacking art should always be condemned, whether it is done in the name of a good cause or not. Art museums are among the few remaining sanctuaries where the public can encounter beauty, complexity, and history in a contemplative space. To violate that space is not only an act against the artwork in question but an affront to the idea of cultural continuity and shared heritage. Just as burning books is not a legitimate way to protest censorship, defacing or attacking paintings is not a legitimate form of climate activism. It is counterproductive, alienating potential allies and reducing complex arguments to mere stunts.

In this context, it is illuminating to consider the case of Ulay, as it is distinctly less (or perhaps even un-) objectionable and it is more clearly an important action-as-artwork, whereas others mentioned here fall far short. His intention was not to destroy or permanently deprive the museum of the artwork but rather to create a symbolic intervention with a deeply considered artistic rationale. Ulay took extensive precautions to ensure the work's safety—filming the act as a performance piece and returning the painting within minutes, unharmed. The work was stolen and returned not as an act of vandalism but as a form of critique—pointing out, in part, the disconnect between what is revered as art and what is neglected in society, such as the poor or marginalized.

Ulay's action may still be considered illegal or controversial, but it operates on an entirely different plane from the recent spate of climate-related art attacks. His gesture was precise, thoughtful, and in dialogue with both the artwork and the institution that housed it. One might still question the ethics of his act, but it is arguably far less objectionable—and perhaps even completely unobjectionable—given its intellectual merit and its respect for the integrity of the painting itself.

The difference is critical. While Ulay's work engages art to make a statement through it, rather than against it, the more recent attacks treat art merely as a stage prop—valuable only for the attention it can draw. Artistic merit, conceptual sophistication, and care for the artwork distinguish legitimate performance or conceptual art from mere spectacle. And that distinction is one we should not lose sight of.

No contemporary artist has weaponized this impulse more effectively—or more mischievously—than Banksy. The anonymous British street artist has built an entire career around interventions that toe the line between crime and critique. Early in his career, Banksy didn't just paint unauthorized murals; he broke into museums to install his own forgeries.

In 2005, visitors to the Brooklyn Museum, the Metropolitan Museum of Art, the Museum of Modern Art, and the American Museum of Natural History encountered unfamiliar works in familiar settings. Banksy had created fake artworks—styled after traditional paintings or scientific exhibits—and hung them on the walls without permission, complete with fake labels.[8] At the MoMA, his piece was a crude portrait of a man in historical garb wearing a gas mask. At the Natural History Museum, it was a stuffed rat with a tiny backpack, displayed as if it were a scientific specimen. Museum security didn't notice. The works remained in place for hours, even days, before being discovered.

The point was not to vandalize but to infiltrate. Banksy's acts of "museum bombing" questioned the gatekeeping function of institutions. If a fake artwork can hang undetected in a major museum, what does that say about the authority of curators and the supposed sanctity of the gallery space? In these acts, the crime is not against the artwork but against the institution itself—a challenge to its power to define, include, or exclude.

In a 2018 stunt at Sotheby's, Banksy took this tactic to its logical conclusion. Moments after his painting *Girl with Balloon* sold for over £1 million at auction, the canvas slid through a shredder hidden in the frame, partially destroying itself in front of a stunned audience. The newly altered artwork, now titled *Love Is in the Bin*, was immediately hailed as a masterpiece of conceptual art—and doubled in value. Here was vandalism as commentary, destruction as creation, and spectacle as market strategy. This was also ingenious, because it was an artist altering his own work and turning it into a unique work of art, distinct from all his other creations and the subject of high-profile media coverage, thereby vastly increasing its value.

These episodes raise complex questions. When is a crime not a crime? When the perpetrator is famous? When the act is documented and declared as art? When the market decides it is valuable? In each of these cases, the artist is both criminal and creator, provocateur and prophet. The act is not an accident but a statement, not damage but discourse.

In such works, the frame becomes a cage, the gallery a battleground. And the question lingers, unanswered: Is the museum a sanctuary—or a stage?

—

What may come as a surprise is that Ulay does not describe the event as a performance, or even as an artwork in the conventional sense. "Action" is the term he favors—*aktion* in German—a word freighted with political, even revolutionary connotations in the postwar German context. Ulay adds the qualifier "demonstrative," emphasizing that the theft was not meant to entertain or mystify but to confront, to agitate, and to communicate.

Were it not for Ulay's status as a major figure in performance and conceptual art, the act would almost certainly be classified as a political protest. That is, in fact, how many newspapers initially framed it. Yet over time, and despite Ulay's own objections, the event has come to be discussed, curated, and canonized as a work of performance art. The question, then, is not simply whether it *is* art but how—and why—it has come to be recognized as such.

Ulay was not the first artist to commit an act of theft in service of a political or artistic agenda. Nor was he the first to do so with the intention of returning the stolen work. The most famous art theft in history—the 1911 heist of the *Mona Lisa*—was also rooted in political symbolism—at least so the thief claimed in court. Vincenzo Peruggia, an Italian handyman and sometime museum worker, removed the painting from the Louvre and smuggled it to his tiny apartment in Paris, believing it had been wrongfully taken from Italy by Napoleon. As is explored in *The Thefts of the Mona Lisa* (2024), while Peruggia may have briefly flirted with the idea of selling the painting, he quickly abandoned the notion and instead attempted to repatriate it to Italy, where he handed it over to the director of the Uffizi Gallery in Florence. The intention, he claimed, was patriotic restitution, not profit.[9]

Peruggia, like Ulay, was a migrant worker who carried an iconic artwork back to a modest room—a gesture charged with cultural and class symbolism. But unlike Ulay, he kept the painting for over two years and made no effort to immediately return it or to explain his motivations until caught. No one then—or now—would categorize his act as art. He never considered it as such. Had he called the police the same day, invited the press, and staged the return, the narrative might have shifted. But as it stands, his act remains a crime, not a cultural gesture.

By contrast, Ulay's "action" has entered the history of contemporary art. A 2008 exhibition at Fort Worth Contemporary Arts in Texas, curated by Gavin Morrison and titled *Lifting: Theft in Art*, examined precisely this phenomenon—when criminal acts overlap with artistic intent.[10] Ulay's theft was its centerpiece, but the show also explored related gestures: from Banksy's illicit graffiti interventions to more controversial acts of vandalism, destruction, or desecration committed in the name of art. Not all such acts carry intellectual weight or artistic merit—many, as Morrison noted, simply provoke without purpose. But Ulay's was different.

Three factors distinguish Ulay's action as art and not mere stunt or protest:

1. The perpetrator was an established artist, already building an international reputation, particularly through his collaborations with Marina Abramović. His identity and intention were inseparable from the meaning of the act.

2. The action was meticulously planned—not only with logistical precision but with a deep awareness of symbolism and spectacle. He composed a fourteen-step plan, mailed a statement to the media (ensuring it would arrive *after* the event), and staged a striking visual gesture by draping a poster-sized reproduction of *The Poor Poet* across the doors of the Academy of Arts. It was a work of art staged as a crime, or a crime staged as a work of art.

3. The event was filmed. Ulay arranged for two perspectives to be captured, as has been covered: one from outside, by cinematographer Jörg Schmidt-Reitwein (who had previously worked with Werner Herzog), and one from within the museum, shot covertly by Abramović. Though her footage lasted only a few seconds, and Schmidt-Reitwein's a matter

of minutes, the act of documentation ensured that the performance would live on—not just in memory or hearsay but as visual, analyzable evidence. As philosopher Peggy Phelan has famously argued, performance art's "only life is in the present," but when it is filmed, it also enters posterity.

Had Ulay not been an artist—had he simply been an activist with a clever idea—this incident would likely have slipped into the footnotes of police archives. Had he not become a world-renowned figure, and had the event not been documented, it would have been forgotten. His rapid confession also complicates legal categorization. He contacted the authorities within minutes of the theft, waited for them to arrive, and made clear that the artwork was unharmed and would be returned.

Under certain legal frameworks, this would not have constituted a prosecutable theft. In the United Kingdom, prior to the 1968 Theft Act, the law required proof of *intent to permanently deprive* the owner in order for an act to be defined as theft. This is what allowed Kempton Bunton, the man who confessed to stealing Goya's *Portrait of the Duke of Wellington* from the National Gallery in 1961, to escape conviction on the primary charge. As detailed in Alan Hirsch's book *The Duke of Wellington Kidnapped* (2021), Bunton admitted to the theft but maintained that he always intended to return the painting, once the government agreed to fund television licenses for pensioners. Because the frame was never returned, Bunton received a minor sentence—but he avoided prison for the more serious crime. After this case, British law was changed to close the loophole.[11]

Had Ulay committed his *aktion* in pre-1968 England, it might not have been legally defined as theft at all.

The line between protest and performance, crime and commentary, is a precarious one. What ultimately elevates Ulay's "Berlin lifting" into the realm of art is not just the idea or the gesture but the identity of the actor, the staging of the act, and its lasting documentation. It was not the first time a painting had been stolen for symbolic reasons. But it was perhaps the first time that such a theft was not a means to an end—but the artwork itself.

And that is what makes it unforgettable.

CAN THEFT BE ART?

The next question—perhaps the most crucial one, and certainly the most debated—is whether Ulay's "Berlin lifting" truly stands up as art. Not as a stunt, a provocation, a crime, or a manifesto, but as a work of art in its own right. Because this is a whole book about the action, you can probably guess that I'll answer in the affirmative. That's not a secret—it is indeed a significant work of art. But why it is considered such is what's really interesting and worth a deeper exploration.

To evaluate that claim, we might begin, paradoxically, by turning back in time—well before performance art, conceptualism, or institutional critique—to the classical roots of aesthetic theory. During the Renaissance, as humanist scholars sought to revive the intellectual traditions of antiquity, one of the foundational texts they turned to was Aristotle's *Poetics*, written in the fourth century BCE. Although Aristotle was writing specifically about poetry and drama, his tripartite definition of what makes a work successful was generalized during the Renaissance into a broader theory of artistic value. According to this adapted Aristotelian model, for a work to be considered a *good* work of art, it must satisfy three essential criteria:[12]

1. It must be good—that is, it must demonstrate skill or excellence in its execution.
2. It must be beautiful—a term derived from the Greek *kalon*, which can mean aesthetically beautiful, morally admirable, or even spiritually uplifting.
3. It must be interesting—it must engage the mind or the emotions; it must provoke thought, curiosity, or attention.

Let us apply these criteria, one by one, to Ulay's action in Berlin.

First: Is It "Good"?

Not in the traditional sense, of course. Ulay did not paint a picture, compose music, or sculpt marble into form. But "goodness" in art does not necessarily mean adherence to a particular medium—it refers to the execution of the idea, the skill with which a work achieves its intended effect. In this sense, Ulay's *aktion* was extraordinarily "good." It was the culmination of careful planning, situational awareness, logistical choreography, and a practiced understanding of space, timing, and public perception. He anticipated the museum's security systems, studied the behavior of guards, identified a legal gray area in fire safety protocols, prepared a getaway vehicle (however unreliable), recruited accomplices, coordinated a film crew, and choreographed a symbolic climax: the installation of *The Poor Poet* in the home of a marginalized immigrant family.

Skill is not always about finesse with a paintbrush. Sometimes it's about how one manipulates context, institutions, and public memory. Ulay's heist was executed with a precision and clarity of purpose that most traditional artworks can only aspire to. As with a tightly composed sonnet or a perfectly timed theatrical monologue, there was no wasted movement.

Second: Is It Beautiful?

Here we must tread more carefully. *Kalon*, the Greek term at the heart of Aristotle's conception, is notoriously slippery. It denotes more than just aesthetic pleasure—it implies a harmony between the external form and an internal virtue. A painting might be *kalon* because of its formal balance but also because it elevates the soul. A noble deed could be *kalon* even if it is not visually pleasing.

So is there beauty in the "Berlin lifting"? Arguably, yes—and in several senses. There is moral beauty in the action's intent: to take an iconic image of German Romanticism, one that had become bound up with nationalist ideology and the shadow of Hitler's admiration, and temporarily repurpose it in a radically different context—hung not in a marble-floored gallery but in the modest living room of a Turkish-German family. This act reclaims cultural symbolism from the institutional and the elite and places it, however briefly, in the space of the everyday, the immigrant, and the marginalized. It is a reversal of aesthetic hierarchy: What was once protected behind glass becomes something like a living object.

There's also a kind of athletic beauty in the act itself. Ulay sprints through the museum, outwits a guard, slips through an emergency exit, navigates a crowd, and plunges into the freezing Berlin streets—all with the painting tucked under his arm. In its own strange way, it's balletic. The performance has the energy of a silent film chase, the grit of a 1970s crime drama, and the structure of a one-act play. It's a performance of motion, risk, and intent. As the filmmaker Chris Marker might say, it is "beautiful because it is fleeting."

Third: Is It Interesting?

This is, perhaps, the easiest of the three to affirm.

Ulay's action continues to spark debate nearly half a century later. It appears in exhibitions, documentaries, academic writing, and classroom discussions—not only in the context of performance art but also in political theory, museum studies, and even criminal law. Its resonance lies in its ambiguity: It is simultaneously an artwork, a theft, a protest, a symbolic inversion, a media spectacle, and a love letter to both cultural critique and conceptual rigor. It asks uncomfortable questions: Who owns culture? Who is allowed to access beauty? What happens when a museum's authority is undermined—not with a bomb or a petition but with a quiet, well-planned act of symbolic mischief?

Furthermore, the fact that Ulay himself resisted calling it art only makes it more compelling. His preference for the term *aktion*—specifically "demonstrative action"—places the work within a lineage of political performance and direct action more than within the art world per se. The German term *aktion* invokes Joseph Beuys, whose "actions" blended shamanism, pedagogy, and provocation. But Ulay's variation is starker, more grounded, less abstract. It doesn't seek transcendence; it seeks confrontation. And the fact that it was carried out with full awareness of its legal, historical, and aesthetic ramifications only sharpens its conceptual edge.

To go further: The very question of whether Ulay's act is "art" *is* part of the artwork. It activates what philosopher Jacques Rancière calls the "distribution of the sensible"—that is, the ways in which art, politics, and perception are arranged and policed in a given culture. By stealing a painting and offering it up in a new context, Ulay destabilized not just the museum but the very category of the artwork. He made us ask: Where is the frame? Who decides what belongs within it?

So by classical standards—skill, beauty, interest—it qualifies. But by modern standards, it may qualify even more powerfully. The action is dialogic: It produces discourse. It is temporal: It occurred in a specific moment but reverberates beyond it. It is site specific: It reacts to the institutions and communities of Berlin. It is participatory: It involves not just the artist but the police, the museum, the Turkish family, the media, and the viewer. And it is documented—preserved on film, in memory, and in scholarship.

If we are willing to accept Marcel Duchamp's urinal as art because it reframes context and authorship, or Yoko Ono's *Cut Piece* because it transforms the audience into coauthors of vulnerability, then we must surely make room for Ulay's "Berlin lifting"—not despite its criminal veneer but because of it. Its legal ambiguity is what makes it conceptually precise. Its illegality is its form.

In the end, perhaps the most Aristotelian thing about Ulay's *aktion* is not the theft, or even the symbolism, but the catharsis. It purges assumptions. It ignites recognition. It gives us, briefly, a vision of what art can still dare to be: not just beautiful but bold, dangerous, and alive.

chapter 8

REMEMBERING **ULAY**

As I write this, at my desk in the Slovenian Alps, I am looking at an all-white brochure that I have simply framed in oak against a white matting. The brochure merely has the words "Retouching Bruises" printed on it—this refers to a photographic series that Ulay created circa 1974, Polaroids in which he photographed himself over the course of several days while repeatedly bruising his face, then attempting to conceal the damage with ever more makeup. Each photograph captures a step in this cycle of harm and repair, exposure (in both senses of the word) and concealment. Ulay's body was the canvas. And instead of signing the brochure to me, he dipped his thumb in lavender-colored ink and pressed it onto the white paper. A signature as thumbprint that looks like a bruise on the page.

It is a strange, lonely thing to write a final chapter about someone you knew, admired, and loved—a chapter that must somehow summarize without ending, eulogize without embalming, and celebrate while grieving. But here we are. Ulay is no longer with us. And yet, in every way that matters, he still is.

He was never *performing* in the shallow sense. He *was*. Even his casual gestures felt curated not for effect but because his whole life had been an action. Not a performance, an *aktion*. That loaded word he favored: an act, a gesture, a strike.

Of course, that most audacious of strikes was *There Is a Criminal Touch to Art*. In some ways, everything that Ulay was or wanted to say is encapsulated in that single act. He did not simply steal a painting. He reclaimed history, disrupted institutional authority, reframed the role of art and the artist. It was a radical, generous crime—not about possession but about confrontation. It made the gallery tremble. It forced the art world to stop and think: Who owns culture? Who decides what matters? And why should that power rest solely in the hands of elites?

This wasn't shock for its own sake. It was ethics in motion. He could have destroyed the painting or kept it, but he didn't. He let the act itself be the message. The moment that frame hit the wall in the immigrants' apartment it became a new artwork. And then, with the cameras rolling, Ulay called the police. There is a reason that I have a section on Ulay on "shock" in my book *The Devil in the Gallery: How Scandal, Shock, and Rivalry Shaped the Art World*.

We talked about that theft many times. It was never a boast. He described it as a civic intervention. A moral realignment. It was performance as protest, art as counterhistory. He was years ahead of everyone else, and the world has only recently caught up to the implications of that act. Banksy owes him a debt. So do we all.

Ulay was, to the end, both fiercely independent and surprisingly tender. He endured hardship with a kind of warrior's quiet. He told me, toward the end, that his cancer ordeal had been "aggressively threatening my life." But he also saw it as part of his life-as-art.

When Ulay was diagnosed with cancer, he did not treat the experience merely as a crisis of health—it became another arena for confrontation, a canvas for reflection, and, perhaps most remarkably, a sort of performance in itself. Not a theatrical one, but a lived, documented action: a *projekt*. He allowed himself to be filmed during the ordeal, opening his life in a way that echoed his artistic principles. The result, *Project Cancer* (2013), directed by

Damjan Kozole, is not a performance artwork in the traditional sense.[1] But it is inseparable from Ulay's identity as an artist whose body was always his primary medium.

From the earliest stages of his career, Ulay had used his body as a site of inquiry and disruption. Whether making up half his face as male and half as female in his *Renais Sense* project, or standing naked in a gallery doorway beside Marina Abramović, forcing viewers to squeeze between them, his physical presence was the vector through which he communicated ideas. So when that body began to fail, to morph, to weaken under chemotherapy, it seemed natural—at least from the outside—to wonder if Ulay would make art of illness.

Indeed, the film's title, *Project Cancer*, evokes the terminology of 1970s performance art—"projects," "actions," and "happenings." It invites a comparison between the unpredictable arc of disease and the structured spontaneity of avant-garde works. Illness, like performance, unfolds in real time, is subject to variables beyond the artist's control, and leaves behind a residue: scars, images, memories, and transformation. One can't help but recall Marina's *Rhythm 0*, in which she surrendered her body to the audience, allowing them to do anything they pleased. What is a more radical surrender than giving your body over to cancer and its treatment?

But if this was ever an idea—if Ulay ever considered turning his illness into a deliberate artistic *aktion*—he wisely abandoned it. The reality was too intimate, too painful, and too real to be staged. Instead *Project Cancer* became something more humble and more profound: a filmed journal of his decline, treatment, healing, and survival. A portrait of an artist whose mind was still razor sharp even as his body trembled. The documentary functions as both personal diary and retrospective, peppered with archival footage and interviews, all framed by his ongoing confrontation with mortality.

Watching the film, I found myself searching for traces of performance— but what emerged was gentler, sadder, and, in its own way, even more honest. There is one line near the end of the film that struck me with particular force. Ulay, gazing out over the Ljubljana skyline from his terrace, says quietly, "This is beautiful." Then he turns toward the camera. "You are beautiful." It was not a line delivered for effect. It was a gift. Even facing death, he was still giving.

That is what he made of his illness: not an artwork but a document of grace under siege. Not spectacle but testament. Not a final act but a quiet continuation. In this, too, Ulay remained an artist to the bone.

There was something almost monastic about his last years. He even ran into Marina at a remote Ayurvedic clinic in India immediately after the two had settled a lawsuit—immediate reconciliation, return to friendship, collaboration . . . this book, coauthored with the two of them, being a fruit of that vine.

Nearer the end, his health was frail but his mind as electric as ever. We spoke, sometimes about potential books, sometimes about nothing at all. He called me "Dear" in every email. He believed deeply in art's ability to do good, to serve, to intervene—not in gallery-speak but in tangible human lives. That is what the Ulay Foundation now exists to preserve. Not just his legacy but his ethos: art that breathes, sweats, bleeds, and listens.

To sit across from him was to sit in a field of magnetic quiet. His highest-profile recent action was simply sitting across from Marina at her MoMA show, a video that has been watched tens of millions of times, so touching does the world find it. He and Marina both told me of their extensive training in meditation that allowed them to remain absolutely still for hours on end as part of their series of performances *Nightsea Crossing* and much later in Marina's *The Artist Is Present*. Ulay had explained how he'd trained himself to "scratch an itch with his mind," which is a magic trick, and how Marina had an advantage in durational seated performances because "my bottom is much bonier than hers." I'll remember him seated—not running into walls so hard that they move. Stillness is power.

I often think of his saying, "Life is absolute. Death is the ultimate answer." And of how he once said that documenting his illness might be the final *aktion*. He wanted even his suffering to serve, not in the martyr sense but because he believed art should reflect life—and life, even in decline, even in decay, had value to show us. He refused to avert his gaze, and he gently asked the world not to either.

This is not an ending. Ulay would hate the idea of being "finished." The point was never the punctuation—it was the action. The *aktion*. And so this book, this last chapter, is a continuation. A gesture toward all the artists who now walk the path he carved with such rawness and grace.

There is, still, a criminal touch to art. Thank God. May Ulay's thumbprint remain all over it.

Selected Bibliography

Biesenbach, Klaus, et al. *Marina Abramović: The Artist Is Present*. Museum of Modern Art, New York, 2010.

Bojan, Maria Rus. "Body: Threshold of Knowledge, Signifying Surface and Generator of Artistic Expression." In *Whispers: Ulay on Ulay*, p. 25.

Bojan, Maria Rus. "Performing Communities: Participatory Aesthetics." In *Whispers: Ulay on Ulay*, p. 43.

Bojan, Maria Rus, and Alessandro Cassin, eds. *Whispers: Ulay on Ulay*. Amsterdam: Valiz, 2014.

Briegleb, Till. "Zum Tod des Künstlers Ulay—Der Alltagsweise." *Frankfurter Allgemeine Sonntagszeitung*, October 16, 2016.

Cassin, Alessandro. "Finding Identity: Unlearning." In *Whispers: Ulay on Ulay*, pp. 189–192.

Charney, Noah. "Ulay Remembers the Crime of a Lifetime 40 Years Later." *Observer*, October 26, 2016.

Debbaut, Jan, ed. *Modus Vivendi: Ulay and Marina Abramović 1980–1985*. Eindhoven: Stedelijk Van Abbemuseum, 1985.

Deumens, Johan. *Ulay: What Is That Thing Called Photography?* Landgraaf: Artists' Books Johan Deumens, 2000.

Harris, Gareth. "Radical Performance Artist Ulay Gets a Solo Show at Stedelijk Museum." *The Art Newspaper*, December 26, 2019.

Iles, Chrissie, and Paul Kokke, eds. *Ulay/Abramović: Performances 1976–1988*. Eindhoven: Stedelijk Van Abbemuseum, 1997.

Kamp, Justin. "Ulay, Pioneering Artist Best Known for Collaborations with Marina Abramović, Dies at 76." *Artsy*, March 2, 2020.

Kozole, Damjan, dir. *Project Cancer: Ulay's Journal from November to November*. 2013.

Krukowski, Samantha. "Performing History: Walking Along Ulay and Abramović's The Lovers." PhD diss., University of Texas at Austin, 1999.

Louisiana Channel. "Ulay Interview: How I Stole a Painting." Video interview.

McEvilley, Thomas. *Art, Love, Friendship: Marina Abramović and Ulay, Together & Apart*. McPherson & Company, 2010.

McEvilley, Thomas, and Irina Grabovan. *Ulay: WE EMERGE*. Art Centre AoRTa, 2004.

McEvilley, Thomas, Tevz Logar, and Marina Abramović. *ULAY: Nastati / Become*. Galerija Škuc, Ljubljana, 2010.

Medien Kunst Netz. "Ulay (Laysiepen, Uwe): Da ist eine kriminelle Berührung in der

Kunst." http://www.medienkunstnetz.de/artist/ulay/biography/.

Morrison, Gavin, and Fraser Staples, eds. *Lifting: Theft in Art*. Atopia Projects, 2009.

Nguyen, Terry. "Ulay and Marina Abramović Turned Love into a Performance." *Vox*, February 11, 2022.

Padtberg, Carola. "Ich habe meine Haut nicht verkauft." *Spiegel Online*, October 13, 2016.

Ruiter, Marita, and Lucien Kayser. *Ulay: Luxemburger Porträts*. Editions Clairefontaine, 1997.

Saito, Ikuo, ed. *Ulay: Berlin/Photogene*. Yamaguchi Prefectural Museum of Art, Kameyama, 1997.

Tate Publishing. *Glam! The Performance of Style*. London, 2013.

Thurman, Judith. "Walking Through Walls." *The New Yorker*, March 8, 2010.

Troost, Frido, ed. *Ulay: Portraits 1970–1993*. Amsterdam: Basalt Publishers, 1996.

Ulrich, Matthias, ed. *Ulay: Life-Sized*. Leipzig: Schirn Kunsthalle Frankfurt, Spector Books, 2016.

Ulay Foundation. https://www.ulayfoundation.org/.

Vignal, Marion. "Portrait de l'artiste en gourou." *Vanity Fair* (France), March 2017.

Westcott, James. *When Marina Abramović Dies: A Biography*. MIT Press, 2010.

Notes

Chapter 2

1   The best book on the subject is Martin Krause, *Carl Spitzweg: The Poor Poet and Other Humorous Paintings* (Indianapolis: Indianapolis Museum of Art, 1992).

2   Rudolf Reiser, *Carl Spitzweg: Der Maler des Biedermeier* (Munich: Langen Müller, 1994), 14–22.

3   Sabine Rewald, *Biedermeier: The Invention of Simplicity* (New York: Metropolitan Museum of Art, 2006), 17–19.

4   For more, see Ulrich Weisstein, *The Essence of Biedermeier* (Indiana University Press, 1974).

5   Wolfgang Maier-Preusker, *Carl Spitzweg: Der arme Poet und seine Zeit* (Vienna: Christian Brandstätter Verlag, 1996), 35–37.

6   Frederic Spotts, *Hitler and the Power of Aesthetics* (New York: Overlook Press, 2002), 11.

7   Brigitte Hamann, *Hitler's Vienna: A Dictator's Apprenticeship* (Oxford: Oxford University Press, 1999), 134.

8   Ian Kershaw, *Hitler: 1889–1936 Hubris* (New York: W. W. Norton, 1999), 43–44.

9   Stephanie Barron, *"Degenerate Art": The Fate of the Avant-Garde in Nazi Germany* (Los Angeles: Los Angeles County Museum of Art, 1991), 9–12.

10 Jonathan Petropoulos, *Artists Under Hitler: Collaboration and Survival in Nazi Germany* (New Haven: Yale University Press, 2014), 78–81.

11 Hector Feliciano, *The Lost Museum: The Nazi Conspiracy to Steal the World's Greatest Works of Art* (New York: Basic Books, 1997), 56–58.

12 Lynn H. Nicholas, *The Rape of Europa: The Fate of Europe's Treasures in the Third Reich and the Second World War* (New York: Alfred A. Knopf, 1994), 133–136.

13 Robert M. Edsel, *The Monuments Men: Allied Heroes, Nazi Thieves, and the Greatest Treasure Hunt in History* (New York: Center Street, 2009), 142–147.

14 Noah Charney, *The Museum of Lost Art* (London: Phaidon, 2018), 97–99.

Chapter 3

1   Ben Quinn and Noah Charney, "Marina Abramović Ex-Partner Ulay Claims Victory in Case about Joint Works," *The Guardian*, September 21, 2016, https://www.theguardian.com/artanddesign/2016/sep/21/ulay-claims-legal-victory-in-case-against-ex-partner-marina-abramovic.

2   This first part of this chapter largely reproduces the homage/obituary I wrote for *The Guardian* following Ulay's passing. It can be viewed at Noah Charney, "'He Stole Hitler's Favorite Painting'—The Naked Genius of My Friend Ulay," *The Guardian*, March 3, 2020, https://www.theguardian.com/artanddesign/2020/mar/03/stole-hitlers-favourite-painting-naked-genius-my-friend-ulay-performance-artist-marina-abramovic.

Chapter 6

1   This chapter is drawn, as the previous accounts were, from my conversations with Ulay and Abramović.

2   Sanders Isaac Bernstein, "Hot Art, Cold Cases: Unsolved Art Theft in Berlin," *The Berliner*, November 21, 2022, https://www.the-berliner.com/art/art-theft-berlin-unsolved-case-francis-bacon-poor-poet-spitzweg-/?utm_.

3   Lisa Beißwanger, "Art Theft as Artwork," *Schirn Kunsthalle Frankfurt*, November 1, 2016, https://www.schirn.de/en/schirnmag/ulay-carl-spitzweg-neue-nationalgalerie-berlin-criminal-touch-art-ulay-context-en/.

4   Noah Charney, *China's Stolen Treasures*, BBC Radio 4, 2022.

5   Charney, *China's Stolen Treasures*.

6   Robert K. Wittman and John Shiffman, *Priceless: How I Went Undercover to Rescue the World's Stolen Treasures* (New York: Crown Publishers, 2010), 222–227.

7   Edward Dolnick, *The Rescue Artist: A True Story of Art, Thieves, and the Hunt for a Missing Masterpiece* (New York: HarperCollins, 2005), 112–117.

8   Ben Macintyre, *The Napoleon of Crime: The Life and Times of Adam Worth, Master Thief* (New York: Delta, 1997), 112–117.

9   Brigitte Hamann, *Hitler's Vienna: A Portrait of the Tyrant as a Young Man*, trans. Thomas Thornton (London: Tauris Parke, 2010), 17–25.

10   For more on Hitler's planned museum and the ERR, see Hanns Christian Löhr, *Kunst als Waffe: Der Einsatzstab Reichsleiter Rosenberg, Ideologie und Kunstraub im "Dritten Reich"* (Berlin: Gebr. Mann Verlag, 2018).

11   Rose Valland, *The Art Front: The Defense of French Collections 1939–1945*, trans. Ophélie Jouan, ed. Robert M. Edsel and Casey L. Shelton (Miller Place, NY: Laurel Publishing, 2024).

12   See Noah Charney, *Stealing the Mystic Lamb* (New York: PublicAffairs, 2010), for more.

13   See Charney, *China's Stolen Treasures*, for more on this section.

14   Alex W. Palmer, "The Great Chinese Art Heist," *GQ*, August 16, 2018.

15   Maggie Kent, "The Vienna Art History Museum Robbery," *Priceless*, December 14, 2022, https://pricelessblog.squarespace.com/articles/the-vienna-art-history-museum-robbery.

16   "Stolen 'Caravaggio' Likely a Copy, Experts Say," *The Local Germany*, June 30, 2010.

17   See Michael Finkel, *The Art Thief: A True Story of Love, Crime, and a Dangerous Obsession* (New York: Alfred A. Knopf, 2023).

18   See Noah Charney, *The Thefts of the Mona Lisa: The Complete Story of the World's Most Famous Artwork* (Lanham, MD: Rowman & Littlefield, 2024), for more.

19   Federal Bureau of Investigation, "Van Gogh Museum Robbery," FBI, https://www.fbi.gov/investigate/violent-crime/art-crime/fbi-top-ten-art-crimes/van-gogh-museum-robbery.

Chapter 7

1   Noah Charney, *Art Crime: Terrorists, Tomb Raiders, Forgers and Thieves* (New York: Palgrave Macmillan, 2009), 9.

2   James E. B. Breslin, *From Word to Image: Art and the Performance of Memory in Postwar America* (Chicago: University of Chicago Press, 2003), 142.

3   Calvin Tomkins, *Off the Wall: A Portrait of Robert Rauschenberg* (New York: Picador, 2005), 204.

4   Sarah Roberts and Katy Siegel, *Rauschenberg* (New York: The Museum of Modern Art, 2017), 46.

5   Tom McDonough, "From Prague to Moscow: Notes on Conceptual Art in Eastern Europe," in *Global Conceptualism: Points of Origin, 1950s–1980s*, ed. Luis Camnitzer, Jane Farver, and Rachel Weiss (New York: Queens Museum of Art, 1999), 102.

6   David Elliott, *Art and Power: Europe under the Dictators 1930–1945* (London: Hayward Gallery, 1995), cited in Andrew Hugill, "Art Crime and Politics: The Case of Alexander Brener," in *Art and Crime: Exploring the Dark Side of the Art World*, ed. Noah Charney (Westport, CT: Praeger, 2009), 153–154.

7   Alex Marshall, "Mashed Potatoes Thrown on a Monet Painting in Climate Protest," *The New York Times*, October 24, 2022, https://www.nytimes.com/2022/10/24/arts/design/monet-painting-mashed-potatoes-climate-protest.html; Philip Oltermann, "Climate Activists Throw Soup at Van Gogh's 'Sunflowers' in London Gallery," *The Guardian*, October 14, 2022, https://www.theguardian.com/environment/2022/oct/14/climate-activists-throw-soup-at-van-goghs-sunflowers-in-london-gallery; Rachel Pannett, "Climate Activists Glue Themselves to Vermeer's 'Girl With a Pearl Earring,'" *The Washington*

Post, October 27, 2022, https://www.washingtonpost.com/world/2022/10/27/climate-protest-vermeer-girl-pearl-earring/.

8   Will Ellsworth-Jones, *Banksy: The Man Behind the Wall* (New York: St. Martin's Press, 2013), 178–181.

9   Noah Charney, *The Thefts of the Mona Lisa: The Complete Story of the World's Most Famous Artwork* (Lanham, MD: Rowman & Littlefield, 2024).

10   Gavin Morrison and Fraser Stables, eds., *Lifting: Theft in Art* (Northampton, MA; Aberdeen, UK: Atopia Projects, 2008).

11   Alan Hirsch, *The Duke of Wellington Kidnapped!* (Seattle: DoppelHouse Press, 2021), 112–117.

12   James S. Ackerman, "The Criteria of Artistic Merit," in *Theory and Design in the First Machine Age*, second edition (Cambridge, MA: MIT Press, 1980), 3–7.

Chapter 8

1   Kozole, Damjan, dir., *Project Cancer: Ulay's Journal from November to November* (Ljubljana, Slovenia: Vertigo, 2013).

Selected Index

These indexed names, places and terms are most important to this story. Ulay's own name has been left out, as it appears on almost every page.

Dr. Noah Charney (b. 1979) is the internationally best-selling author of more than thirty books, translated into fourteen languages, including *The Collector of Lives: Giorgio Vasari and the Invention of Art*, which was nominated for the 2017 Pulitzer Prize in Biography, and *Museum of Lost Art*, which was the finalist for the 2018 Digital Book World Award. He is a professor

About the Author

of art history specializing in art crime and has taught at Yale University, Brown University, American University of Rome, and University of Ljubljana. He is the founder of ARCA, the Association for Research into Crimes against Art, a groundbreaking research group (www.artcrimeresearch.org), and teaches on their annual summer-long Postgraduate Program in Art Crime and Cultural Heritage Protection. He has written for dozens of major magazines and newspapers, including *The Guardian*, *The Washington Post*, *The Observer*, and *The Art Newspaper*. He writes for TED and presents on television and radio, including a BBC series called *China's Stolen Treasures* and programs for The Great Courses. This is his twelfth book with Bloomsbury/Rowman & Littlefield; his other books include *The Devil in the Gallery: How Scandal, Shock and Rivalry Shaped the Art World*; *Making It: The Artist's Survival Guide*; *The 12-Hour Art Expert: Everything You Need to Know About Art in a Dozen Masterpieces*; *Gold Wine*; *The NFT Book: Everything You Need to Know about the Art and Collecting of Non-Fungible Tokens*; *Brushed Aside: The Untold Story of Women in Art*; *The Thefts of the Mona Lisa: The Complete Story of the World's Most Famous*

Artwork; *Forgers & Thieves*; *The 12-Hour Film Expert*; *The Art of Fatherhood*; *The Accidental Picasso Thief*; *Empower Your Kids*; and *The 12-Hour Author*. He lives in Slovenia with his wife, children, and their hairless dog, Hubert van Eyck. Learn more at www.noahcharney.com.